LOTUSLAND
A PHOTOGRAPHIC ODYSSEY
text by Theodore Roosevelt Gardner II

CONTENTS

History	16
The Gardens	22
House Area	26
Cacti—Succulents	34
Ferns	48
Aloes	54
Blue Garden	68
Japanese Garden	72
Water Gardens	80
Palms	90
Cycads	96
Ganna Walska	106
The Husbands	112
Walska's Interests	122
Ganna Walska Builds Her Garden	129
Additional Photo Captions	138
Photographer Credits	140
Acknowledgements	141
Index	142
In Memory	144

ALLEN A. KNOLL, PUBLISHERS

Copyright and CIP data found on page 141

(Left): The house Ralph Kinton Stevens built in 1893.

HISTORY

It was a land grant from the U.S. Government in 1877. Wild and woolly until then, Montecito was scrub oaks and chaparral and sturdy, plodding native oaks which survived drought and deluge. The first few owners kept it that way.

It was the sixth owners (in six years), Ralph Kinton Stevens and his wife Caroline, who named the ninety-eight acres Tanglewood, in honor of the nettlesome tangle they found covering their new homestead. And the Stevenses set out to untangle the woods, selling off parcels until they were left with the thirty-seven acres we know today as Lotusland.

Ganna Walska was fortunate in her predecessor; Kinton Stevens, with his exotic-plant nursery, gave her a running start. He planted *Jubaea chilensis*, the fat-trunked Chilean wine palms over a hundred years ago, making them the largest specimens in the United States. He began the lotus pond and the lotuses he planted were still alive when she began her contributions seventy-five years later.

(Below): View from across Sycamore Canyon Road, south of property, facing north, c. 1890s. Lemon trees are planted in the foreground at the right.

The Stevens family got into lemons and sold many trees to neighboring orchards. The trouble was everyone in the Montecito Valley was soon in lemons, up to their necks, and there was no more market for lemons. In the West, everyone had them, and in the East, they got them cheaper from Italy, where they came across the ocean as ballast for ships.

Getting water to irrigate the crops was a horrendous undertaking. First they tried windmills, but they didn't produce a sufficient flow of water to meet their needs. Then Stevens built a reservoir—now used as the pond in the Japanese garden. As his nursery business grew, he had to find more water. He bored large tunnels in the mountain rock, a task carried out by two Chinese laborers he favored.

The city commandeered his water source in a dry year, but Kinton Stevens struggled on. Perhaps the hardships of the pioneers crushed his heart, but they never touched his spirit, which was said to be unflinchingly good-natured. He was a man who was beloved by all and never heard to raise his voice.

He filled his short life with horticultural accomplishment that would have done credit to a man with twice his life span.

He planted many varieties of fruit trees, along with the early main lemon crop. He befriended officers of trading vessels that occasionally docked in Santa Barbara. In return for his many kindnesses, packages of seed and bundles of green cuttings would come to Stevens from South Africa, Australia, the East Indies, and any other countries the ship would visit with compatible climates.

(Above): Sycamore Canyon Road entry c. 1910, where entry gate is today. Sign on left says, "Open to Guests Only". Palm trees are the fat-trunked Jubaea chilensis, *the Chilean wine palms, planted by Kinton Stevens, c. 1880s.*

(Left): Kinton Stevens's children loved to go row boating on their "lake". This reservoir with Lotus plants is now the Japanese garden pond, c. 1897.

(Below): Early Idria columnaris *and cactus plantings*

His exotic-plant nursery soon flourished and he was not only supplying his Montecito and Santa Barbara neighbors with unique palms and other exotics, but he began a successful catalogue business as well.

The Stevenses lived in the then-existing house until they moved it into the oak trees and built their own house of stone and wood in 1893.

Kinton Stevens made his garden into one of the great gardens in the West. People came from miles around to see it, just as they do to Lotusland today.

He became a preeminent nurseryman of his time, visiting Hawaii in 1891 to collect plants for the San Francisco Golden Gate Park.

Mankind was deprived of his services suddenly when he was struck down with a heart attack in 1896, at the age of forty-eight.

(Above): The original swimming pool between water gardens; now the Lotus pond
(Left): Olive Allée

The next owners to make major changes were the Erastus Palmer Gavits. They took possession in 1916 and renamed Tanglewood, Cuesta Linda, Spanish for "pretty hill." They built the walls surrounding the property, and in 1920 built the large Spanish stucco house that exists today.

They are responsible for the bathhouse, olive *allée* in back, as well as the Moorish fountain, the water stairs, the parterre and formal gardens.

Ralph T. Stevens, son of Kinton, initially helped the Gavits revitalize his father's gardens.

Looking north to house and mountain, c. 1941

Aerial views:
(Left): c. 1920s
(Below): from north, c. 1970, new swimming pool is at bottom right, house middle right

(Right): Bamboo at Lotusland, mid-century.

Humphrey Clarke held the property for about a year before selling it to Madame Ganna Walska in 1941. She began immediately to take an interest in the garden, which she called Tibetland. When she was free of her sixth and final husband in 1946, she concentrated all her commanding energies on her garden. She quickly renamed the property Lotusland.

Over the years, a scant few over a century in cultivation, Lotusland has undergone manifold mutations. From the chaparral and scrub oaks, to lemon and fruit trees, to eucalyptus groves and exotic palms—there was even a time when bamboo thrived on the acreage—to the eclectic mix of Ganna Walska's particular genius for amassing species, the garden has been touched by magic hands, and magic is the result.

(Above): Aerial view, 1993
(Above Right): Nelumbo nucifera (Lotus)
(Left): View from back of main house (on the right), c. 1920s. Ganna Walska lived in the pavilion on the left.

THE CHAIN OF TITLE

1877   A ninety-eight acre homestead grant from U.S. Government to CHARLES NEWBOLD sold to JOHN CROSS for $3,800.

1879   CROSS deeded it back to NEWBOLD NEWBOLD sold to BURKILL JACQUES

1881   M.A. MAUFAIR

1882   RALPH KINTON STEVENS

1887   STEVENS sold northern half to CHARLES EATON

1894   STEVENS sold another parcel, keeping the thirty-seven acres that remain today. He called his property TANGLEWOOD.

1913   GEORGE OWEN KNAPP

1916   ERASTUS PALMER GAVIT. Built house and walls around 1920. Renamed the property *Cuesta Linda* (Pretty Hill).

1940   HUMPHREY CLARKE

1941   GANNA WALSKA named it *TIBETLAND*

1946   GANNA WALSKA renamed it *LOTUSLAND*

1984   GANNA WALSKA LOTUSLAND FOUNDATION

The life of Ganna Walska was a life of the opera. Many of the mysteries of her life are buried in her pursuit of operatic fame. "Opera" is the Latin plural for the word "opus," meaning work. Musical compositions are numbered for composers by opus number. Opera is many works. It is music, drama, art and spectacle. It is the most "operatic" opus. The most multifaceted work of art.

The rhythms of the opera were more influential than was the ticking of the clock or the turning of the calendar. Color, harmony, drama and spectacle moved her. So we will begin at the house which served as the nerve center for her operation and fan out from there as the music and drama lead us. Like she would have let the spirit move her.

THE GARDENS

In this eclectic garden you feel the opera all around. Each garden is a stage setting. Each chorus of plants is reminiscent of some opera or other: *Rigoletto* in the aloe garden, *Carmen* in the lotus pond, and *Madame Butterfly*, of course, in the Japanese garden.

When her younger ambitions for preeminence on the opera stage were behind her, as the memory of the last unhappy marriage began to fade, Madame Ganna Walska was able at last to throw herself into her final quest to make a difference in the world.

With single-minded devotion, she dedicated over forty years to the designing, planting and nurturing of her spectacular garden. Then she endowed it so that others might take pleasure in it.

The gardens depicted here are in no particular order. Not chronological, based on their initial designs, because there are many crossovers. Madame Ganna Walska did not seem to be scientifically or chronologically oriented. She was an artist. Beauty was her bounty.

The original house was designed by Reginald Johnson and built in 1919-1920. It was later remodeled with the help of the celebrated George Washington Smith, who gets credit also for the bathhouse at the lotus pond (former swimming pool).

Euphorbia and cactus plantings existed when Ganna Walska bought the property in 1941. They were too sparse for her taste. So, she augmented them with

HOUSE AREA

The tortured *Euphorbia ingens,* twisting and turning their way to the heavens and, as though having second thoughts, back again, give the home a Halloweenish quality. It is one of the most photographed aspects of Lotusland, and has helped make the house instantly recognizable to anyone who has seen it before.

masses of cacti surrounding her living quarters—the pavilion off to the south side of the main house where she stored her considerable furnishings and collections, but where she never lived.

In the front traffic circle is crammed an army of *Dracaena draco,* popularly known as dragon trees. They have grown so tall and thick the area underneath is plunged in perpetual darkness.

Out back, the vast lawn is bordered by so many varieties of plants. There is the huge Monterey cypress (*Cupressus macrocarpa*) which Kinton Stevens couldn't sell when he had his nursery business one hundred years ago. The tree was apparently forgotten and the roots, as if in revenge for the neglect, jumped out of the box and dove into the ground, where they plunged deeper and deeper, sending the rest of the tree high in the sky, until it towered over the house itself.

The tree is now so beloved, extensive wiring has been done to hold it all together, lest it breaks apart from weight and age.

This area of the garden has several native oaks, and under these grand, spreading oak trees Madame Walska has planted bromeliads in raised beds—a daring feat considering the sensitivity of oaks to summer watering. This is successfully overcome by light, judicious watering and results in a striking effect.

A further stroll down the lawn brings you to a herd of elephants' feet, the troop of ponytail palms—the *Beaucarnea recurvata*—with the swollen trunk bases that look like elephant feet. Did they remind Madame Ganna Walska of spectacular productions of *Aïda* with a stage full of camels and elephants?

In Ganna Walska's time, you would have seen magnificent topiary animals on the lawn. And she had them before Walt Disney did.

The large planted clock was a favorite of the proprietress. But it was a constant struggle to keep the number markers, and the decorative twelve signs of the zodiac, from being stolen. Finally, after making several replacements, she gave the clock a gravel face.

(Top left): Beaucarnea recurvata, 1994
(Top middle): Main house from patio with Olea europaea (olive) in foreground
(Top right): Lemon arbor

(Above): The giant clock with the signs of the zodiac and numerals, c. 1950s

(Left): Topiary animals at Lotusland during Ganna Walska's time, 1958
(Right): mosaic path

At the far end of the lawn is her theater garden, where she staged some musical events, and doubtless dreamed of countless others. Did she ever dream of performing in this sylvan theater? Probably not. She seemed content to have traded her music-making for garden-making.

The theater, which now serves mainly the imagination of those who see it, has a permanent audience in the form of an enlightened group of concrete grotesques which Madame brought from her French château. Though the dwarf men provide a loyal and dependable audience, they do not seem to be an appreciative one.

But any way you look at them, they are great stone faces, and might have reminded Ganna Walska of some members of her own audiences. Or perhaps they represent her view of her critics.

The parterre has gone through several mutations. The fountains used to have fresh-flowing water. This is a scandalous thought in the era of heightened environmental consciousness, and drought awareness. All water elements on the property are now recirculating.

The fruit orchard, olive *allée* and rose garden have undergone slight changes from their original state pre-Ganna Walska.

The lawn area could be the slow movement of the symphony. A time to contemplate—the only truly open space in the garden, where the senses are given leave of the need to grasp everything in sight.

CACTI - SUCCULENTS

The cacti and euphorbias are prick-prickly plants, much better to look at than to touch. They beg you to keep your distance. Madame surrounded her residence with these forbidding sentries. She might have wanted to be a little standoffish. They would help.

And she planted them in regiments, like an opera chorus with swords at the ready.

These spiny, injurious, drought-tolerant plants were her first collecting interest. She didn't want one of each, she wanted lots of each.

When Ganna Walska began her ambitious garden plantings, she added to the sparse existing desert plants around the house a thousandfold—and as though coming alive, these sturdy plants marched south down the driveway to their own territory.

Here are endless ranks of a hundred cactus pipe organs, all satisfied with their space, comfortable in their thorny skins.

The cactus garden ends in the succulents, fleshy plants that hold liquid to keep them alive when there is no water to feed them. They are camels of the plant kingdom.

The euphorbias across the street are often indistinguishable from the cacti; the euphorbias have a poisonous milky liquid in them which if gotten on the skin can cause severe discomfort.

Back in front of the house, you see the twisting *Euphorbia ingens* and the *Echinocactus grusonii*, the golden barrel cactus, amusingly nicknamed "Mother-in-law's cushion".

In the circle in front of the house are the giant *Dracaena draco*, leading on to the fern gardens. These unique specimens, related to agaves, are from the Canary Islands, and the resin of some species is called dragon's blood and is used in varnish and photoengraving. Hence their popular name, dragon trees.

36

39

The paths meander in the fern garden. It is a meandering, moseying kind of place. Ferns put you in mind of a slow shuffle—unruffled, unhurried. They are arching with foliage soft like a cashmere sweater. The fern garden is the jade of Madame's gemstones—not too rare, but not common either.

Ferns have smooth lines and a gentle, easy transition from one plant to the other, as though they were folding into each other. They are the antithesis of the cacti.

The dry environment of Southern California is not generally hospitable to ferns, so an environment conducive to them must be maintained. Deep shade and lots of moisture make ferns happy. At its peak, you should get a grotto feeling moseying among the ferns. The fern gardens were created and re-created during Ganna Walska's lifetime, and extended after she died. She initially resisted adding the colorful begonias, but then embraced the idea.

FERNS

Some garden writers consider aloes ugly plants. Their thick leaves have jagged edges as inviting as broken glass. Most of them stay close to the ground, like hermits daring you to touch them.

The colors of their fleshy aloes' leaves vary widely, from yellows and bright greens, to dull reds, scarlet, blue and the

ALOES

ubiquitous gray. And the bursts of winter color are operatic—flaming reds, luminous yellows, oranges and magenta burst from the thick leaves, bringing bright cheer to the gloomy, somber days of winter. When in full bloom, the aloe garden can put you in mind of the merriest of Christmases.

Imagine Ganna Walska standing by the flaming aloes just after a rain, studying the luminous leaves through the droplets of water reflecting the splashes of color from the flowers above. They must have reminded her of her jewels catching the light just so—glimmering, shimmering, sparkling.

And maybe she cast her memory back to the perpetual gray of St. Petersburg in Russia, where she made her first trek from home. How happy it would have made her then to have these glorious flaming flowers to pierce that unalterable gloom.

It was in her aloe garden that Ganna Walska rimmed her pond with the shiny, pearly abalone shells which evoke cries of "kitsch" in some and "eclectic" in others.

Was the shell pond her opera buffa? At least it should get high marks for buffoonery. It does seem perfect for cooking up a witches' brew for Verdi's *Macbeth*. Or for staging the sorcery in Wagner's *Parsifal* and Saint-Saëns' *Samson and Delilah*. Was the great lady teasing us?

An inside joke perhaps—like the scherzo of a symphony. It is probably the most photographed and talked-about feature of Madame's garden; and who knows, she may have planned it that way. Her life was one of doing the unusual. She took pride in it.

And we should not forget the celebrated tenor aria in *Rigoletto*, "La Donna è Mobile" in which the duke expresses his opinion that all women are fickle.

"Blue" is a gratifying word to sing. A light plosive "B" followed by the liquid "L" and the soothing, soft vowel "ooooo." When you think how musical the word "blue" is, you wish more operas were sung in English.

But the blue garden at Lotusland sings. It reflects the color of the sky, and the special feeling the blue garden gives is more in the soothing true-blue context than the depressed, low-spirited meaning of the word.

The word "blue" has been so aptly used in concert with other common words to describe the less common: blue moon, blue cheese, bluegrass, union blue, blue

BLUE GARDEN

laws. Or it evokes feelings, as in singing the blues. It is used to categorize people sartorially as in bluestocking, blue blazer, bluebottle, bluejacket, bluegown; or to set apart by social class: bluebook, bluenose; or merely to recognize as important, as in blue ribbon.

Now it distinguishes a section of the Lotusland garden adjacent to the lawn, devoted to plants with blue foliage. Here, underfoot, is the Blue fescue (*Festuca ovina v. glauca*). At about knee to waist height you can see *Agave americana* and *Agave franzosinii*. At eye level, some smaller *Brahea armata* (Blue hesper palms), and overhead, the Atlas cedar (*Cedrus atlantica cv. glauca*).

All this blue could sap your spirits. But instead of making you feel blue, the blue garden envelopes you in a calming, secure container of contentment, as though you just came home to your own corner of the sky.

JAPANESE GARDEN

Dear Maidens, I hastened here at the call of my heart!
— Madame Butterfly

It was Ganna Walska's favorite garden, they say, and no wonder. *Madame Butterfly* seems to have been Madame's favorite opera. She had extraordinary costumes made for the part.

Here in the Japanese garden one can easily imagine Madame in a costume of the lacy *Chusquea coronalis* bamboo or the delicate leaves of the *Salix babylonica* the weeping willow tree.

This garden is more lyrically attuned to the soft ferns than it is to the jagged aloes and prickly cacti. It is a place perfect for repose, for absorbing the quiet sounds of gently moving water, for luxuriating in the plants indigenous to the reticent gardens of Japan.

The artistically shaped Japanese black pine (*Pinus thunbergiana*), the lonely maple (*Acer palmatum*), the *Nandina domestica* (the Heavenly bamboo, which is not bamboo at all), the water brimming with lotuses to the island of *Cycas revoluta*, the Sago palm (not a palm either), all plants to put you at peace.

The scale is large—much larger than the traditional delicate Japanese gardens with a few, well-placed rocks in the raked sand, and perhaps a *Pinus thunbergiana* or two. But Madame Ganna Walska did not think small; she did things on a large scale, and her Japanese garden was no exception.

Madame Butterfly is a tragic opera. Cio-Cio-San, the young Japanese girl ("Madame Butterfly") who gives herself to an American naval officer, comes to a tragic end. There are moments of joy, as well as sadness; hope, as well as despair.

Here in Walska's Japanese garden we stand and look down at the water and hear Butterfly singing to her baby:

...Oh, listen, good people,
Listen for the love of the all eight
hundred thousand gods
and goddesses of Japan!

76

WATER GARDENS

Here is the namesake of the garden, the *Nelumbo nucifera*, popularly known as the lotus, the name adopted by Madame Ganna Walska for her garden in 1946, after her divorce from the "White Lama," for whom she had named it Tibetland.

The stunning lotus is a metaphor for so many things. It represents fertility, beauty, sexuality, steadfastness, love, regeneration, resurrection, spiritual transcendence, and more. It is a uniquely beautiful plant, with striking leaves, translucent petals and golden core; even the pods have glorious proportions. Here, some of the most delightful and artistic pictures in the garden have been taken. Note how each of the photographers captured various lights and turned them to artistic advantage.

The name Lotusland reflects Madame Walska's desire that her gardens be a place of tranquility and spiritual renewal...Inspired by the victory of the lotus flower, Madame Walska gradually turned away from a highly social life and vocal performance to at last find expression of her 'purpose'—that for which all the good and bad in her life had prepared her. A lasting symbol from nature for the transcendence of the soul above the physical world and all of its suffering, the lotus remains for us today a symbol of Madame Walska's keen interest in advancing her soul towards *nirvana*.

—Janet M. Eastman
Historical Symbolism of the Lotus

Perhaps the most striking thing about the lotus is its growth habit. These lovely plants rise from the mud of the pond bottom, then push their leaves above the water level and spew forth the most spectacular blooms in the summer sun. Two thousand years ago, the Egyptians thought the sun sprang from the lotus plant. Great beauty from humble beginnings? A metaphor for dozens of operas—and perhaps for Madame herself.

Other water plants are the common, but also radiantly beautiful, water lily (*Nymphaea caerulea*, blue; and *Nymphaea lotus*, night-blooming white flower) and the exotic, outsized *Victoria regia* lily (Royal or Amazon water lily). The lotuses occupy the lake in the Japanese garden, as well as the rectangular former swimming pool in front of the bathhouse. On both sides of the lotuses are large water lily ponds.

> The aquatic lotus is unrelated to the lotus mentioned by Homer in the *Odyssey*. In that 8th c. B.C. epic poem, Odysseus and his men on their voyage home from the Trojan War stopped at an island called the Land of the Lotus-Eaters. Here his men ate the lotus, some kind of a fruit, nut or flower with a narcotic effect, which caused them to forget about home and wish only to remain on the island and eat more lotus…
>
> The term "lotus land" came to describe any fabulous, dreamlike setting from which one wished never to return. It became a slang term for Hollywood and its film industry—an unreal world of illusion and dreams. Though many have characterized Madame Walska's Lotusland in this light, emphasizing the unreal quality of her gardens, this may not be what Ganna Walska intended…it seems more likely that she intended to evoke the sacred ideas related to the aquatic lotus and to characterize her own spiritual path which culminated in her dedication to creating a thing of beauty which would last forever.
>
> —Janet M. Eastman
> *Historical Symbolism of the Lotus*

The palms have grown so big in their dramatic bunches that their leaves are competing for the scarce space in the sky.

Kinton Stevens's catalogue in 1893 featured many plants that were rare in this country one hundred years ago. He listed *Butia*, *Pritchardia*, *Phoenix*, *Sabal* and *Livistona* species among other genera, including one named the *Stevensonia grandiflora*, which we know now as *Phoenicophorium borsigianum*. The leftovers were a fortuitous foundation for the palm collection at Lotusland.

A lot of these palms were at eye level when Madame Ganna Walska put them in. You could look down on the leaves of some of them. Now you'd need a helicopter to see the tops of these majestic, arching beauties. From the ground it is now mostly trunks and the undersides of the proud fronds.

Some of the most dedicated (not to say fanatical) plantsmen are the palm enthusiasts, sometimes amusingly referred to as palm nuts.

Madame Walska played hostess to the Palm Society, and a few weeks before the event, was thrown into a state of panic. She was convinced her palm collection was inadequate for the group. So she bought dozens more specimen palms and had them installed in time for the gathering.

By the time she finished there were more than 375 of these mature trees, and sixty species in the garden.

CYCADS

The cycads are Ganna Walska's rarest gemstones, the zillion-carat diamond she hung around her neck when she wanted to make an impression.

The plants are not flashy, but they are expensive. They are slow growing, but generally hardy and reliable. Like diamonds.

This comparison is apt, since Ganna Walska said she sold the last big batch of her jewelry for close to a million dollars to finance her cycad collection.

And here, at last, we come to the waltz in Madame's garden. Try to think of Lotusland without its peerless cycad collection. It is simply one of the outstanding collections of these rare, fossil plants in the world. And the rarest of the rare, the *Encephalartos woodii*, which are no longer known to exist in the wild, are represented here not with a forlorn single plant—not with a pair—but with THREE! As in three-quarter time, Madame Walska's greatest waltz. And they aren't puny seedlings either, but mature specimens hovering around six feet tall. And the seeds necessary for prolonging the species no longer exist.

There are only eleven genera of cycads, and nine are represented here. They look to many like small palm trees. Plants whose leaf tops you can see for decades. But they are unrelated to the majestic palms, which have flowers. Cycads have cones, like pine trees.

And they are so magnificently displayed here, on mounds, in valleys, by a soothing pond, each given room to breathe and prosper. It takes a rare expert to tell these striking plants apart. It often comes down to how many tiny jagged protrusions there are on the leaflets, and how they are arranged. But if you possess that expertise, the rare fossil plants are placed so you can see even these minutest of details.

It is not difficult to imagine Ganna Walska's pride in this garden. It was the capstone of her career, completed toward the end of her life. Not many people had cycads, she noted, and that pleased "the enemy of the average."

Ganna Walska

A handwriting analyst might say the obvious things about Ganna Walska's signature: flamboyant, artistic, bold. There might even be a suggestion she was larger than life.

Leaving her family and what she referred to as a strict Roman Catholic upbringing behind, she left home at a tender teen age to make her way in a foreign country. Once gone, she never looked back. She broke with every tradition she could. She was a maverick, strong-willed and focused, and with virtually her will and personality alone she amassed a respectable fortune, had six husbands when her church forbade divorce, struggled for preeminence in a career for which she didn't seem suited, and built one of mankind's horticultural monuments in her garden in Lotusland.

She was a pillar of perseverance. "I didn't give up" was one of her favorite sayings. Napoleon Bonaparte said, "Victory goes to the persevering." And she was that. Her father was also named Napoleon, and his only daughter was not without her own warlike qualities.

The story of Madame Ganna Walska is one of the great stories of our day. She was a personality with a style that encouraged myths. Some of them she perpetuated herself, some she abhorred.

But during her ninety-seven years, she was constantly talked about.

She was a woman of stunning beauty, boundless nervous energy, and enviable accomplishments. She had a gift for marrying wealthy men, but no talent for staying married. She was a genius at getting generous sums of money settled on her and was able to parlay the first four of her marriages into the gold mine that financed Lotusland.

She devoted some twenty-five years of her life pursuing a career as an opera star, taking daily lessons from a variety of teachers, practicing hour after hour, attending performances with religious regularity.

Listening to a recording of Ganna Walska singing, one is struck by the wide and erratic vibrato and the pitch at variance with the piano accompaniment. The timbre of the voice could benefit from more resonance. One's heart goes out to this driven woman who devoted a lifetime to being an opera star with a voice that would not ordinarily have landed her a place in the chorus. But she never gave up the dream of conquering an opera audience, not with her always-provocative, sometimes-outlandish costumes and spectacular jewels, not with her incredible beauty, but with her *voice*.

She was a kaleidoscope of shifting patterns, spectacular and elusive; an eclectic eccentric; a contrivance of contradictions.

She started life as Hanna Puacz in Brest-Litovak, Poland.

She was her father's middle child, and only girl; her mother's youngest. After her mother, Carolina, died and Napoleon remarried, Hanna had two half-brothers. The Puaczes were landowners, not kings and queens, but not peasants either.

In 1943, Ganna Walska published a rambling autobiography, *Always Room at the Top*. In it, she deftly obscures her birthdate. The most convincing documentation sets the date as 1887.

Carolina and Napoleon Puacz

Hanna Puacz with her father in Poland, c. 1897

Ganna Walska was a woman often guided by fantasies and attracted to myths. Her name is a fantasy. Anna and Ganna (and Hanna) mean "divine." She liked to dance, so she called herself the Divine Waltz (Walska was her name for "waltz").

> In those days a married woman could not have her name appear in print—she dared not even have her address on her visiting cards—so I was not about to use my husband's name at an occasion when I was to sing for charity. At the eleventh hour I had to think up a substitute and, like all Poles, I loved to dance, especially to waltz. So suddenly I said: "Waltz, Valse, Walska...!
> —Ganna Walska
> —*Always Room at the Top*

Or so she said. What is less generally known is that Napolean Bonaparte had a mistress of Polish royal blood who bore him a child. Her name was Madame Walweska. Could Hanna Puacz have appropriated the first three and last three letters of this name as her own? Remember her father's name was Napolean.

Should we give credence to her story that she started singing to attract the attention of a very rich man associated with opera, a Russian royal who expressed no interest in her? It is a story that would conform to her character. But day in and day out, through four marriages?

She claimed the name change was dictated by the social mores of the time, but after the performance she clung to it for the rest of her life, through five more husbands and fifty years in America.

Madame Ganna Walska!

Perhaps she had a point. Hanna Puacz Lotusland had less music. And music was in her bones. Her gardens brim with melody and harmony. And the seductive rhythms of dance. She was a divine waltzer. Not in any oom-pah-pah sense, but rather, dah da *daaah*, da da *daah*; Viennese not German. The kind of waltz you do in silk flowing gowns and satin buckle shoes to a dozen violins at court—not in lederhosen to a brass band in a beer hall.

And the Divine Waltz called herself "Madame." A funky pretension in this country in these times, but to her it embodied the respect she felt she had earned.

When an opera director in Cuba called out, "Walska!" to her, she corrected him: "*Madame* Walska if you please!"

She said he replied, "We don't call Caruso, *Mr.*—it's Caruso. You should be different?"

She claimed that made her feel small, but she didn't drop the "Madame." She was not a quitter.

In her middle years, with virtually unlimited means at hand, she turned to society. She liked the feeling of doing good she got by bringing forth in her famous musical salons great young talents.

Here, among her friends and protégés, she could forget the harsh criticism of her own abilities and revel in the association of those on whom the critics bestowed their kindest thoughts. Paramount among these young musical hopefuls, she mentions Vladimir Horowitz, the renowned Russian pianist.

"I caught a glimpse of Ganna Walska at the Alsen recital. She was a radiant apparition in a costume of jade velvet with a hat of the same material and the whole speaking well of Parisian ateliers. Most women in this imperfect world would be more than content to look like that, and would gladly forswear any desire to sing..."

—*Unattributed newspaper account of Madame Ganna Walska*
—*quoted in* Always Room at the Top *as an insult to her intelligence*

Letter from antique dealer Christian Rub, 12/10/47

MY VERY DEAR FRIEND: This is my "Goodbye-letter" to you and my "last wish" is not to call you "Madame" as this is too cold and formal and besides it always reminds me of a midwife, which is always called "die Madameeee". I had to call you as the old Antiqueshop-Dealer, with that certain (outside) respect "Madame", but now I am free and "unclassified" and can do how I please and so I call you: MY VERY DEAR FRIEND. And you really have been a very good friend to us, not only an important "stockholder" of this forced Antique Adventure but an adorable personality, even when you were very severe and despotic, I never took you serious, because I am pretty smart and I could look through you quite well and enjoyed every minute with that sparkling, spoiled, fascinating and a little bit crazy (thanks god) Ganna.

(Above): Ganna Walska crossing the Atlantic on the Île de France.

> I would analyze my case thoroughly and if with each daily lesson I would give myself another chance and another chance, still with all the lucidity at my disposal I knew it was useless, it was hopeless...Coolly I would speak to myself as an elderly person would speak to a child:
>
> "Do not be obstinate!! You cannot do it! Wherefore then continue this suffering? Wherefore these ceaseless agonies?"
>
> "Very well," my alter ego would answer, "I *cannot* sing—but then how can I exist? Life without work is unthinkable to me!"
>
> —Ganna Walska
> —*Always Room at the Top*

(Above): Ganna Walska visiting in Idaho, c. 1942, about the time she acquired Lotusland.

(Below): Ganna Walska hosting a party at Lotusland.

And when she came into the room you noticed her. Her eclectic dresses and original hats, her ponderous and priceless jewelry could not fail to catch your eye. If that didn't do it, the twinkle in her eye and the pixie grin took over. She said she never flirted. Others would say flirting was ingrained in her nature. Could anyone get six husbands and untold proposals being a wallflower?

Interspersed in her memoirs is a recurring quest for the meaning of life. This Roman Catholic widened her search. She studied Eastern religions and gained a Buddhist lama for her sixth husband.

Countless portraits were painted of her, numerous busts of her likeness sculpted, and thousands of photographs were taken, all attesting to her legendary beauty.

It was a burden she bore admirably until near the end, when she directed the executors of her will "that upon my passing away, my body be concealed from view of all..."

If, in spite of biblical admonitions to the contrary, you must judge her, you may be pulled to one extreme or the other:

You may consider her a philanthropist, a forerunner of the feminists, who stood up to the men in her life and got her fair share of their worldly goods. After all, men had been using and discarding women for centuries. She was just getting back at men for brutes like Henry VIII, or perhaps she was just a hopelessly incurable romantic who adored men who could never live up to her idolization of them; a strong woman who knew her mind and knew how to get what she wanted and was not afraid to go after it on any avenue, whether open to her or not. Struggling against odds, persevering, tenacious, with taste and panache. A magnetic woman, poised and self-possessed, generous to a fault, who could turn adversity to advantage at the flick of a bejeweled finger. An astute businesswoman and struggling artist employing the advantages of wealth.

She came out of Poland with negligible financial resources—took Russian royalty by storm, wowed the French musical elite, then swept America off its feet; all admittedly done with a thin musical capital. And she died a multimillionaire.

Or you might think of her as avaricious: a conniving, cunning woman, using men to her advantage. Deserting each of her six husbands for her own selfish aims. A woman of questionable ethical sense, leading on her fourth husband while married to her second (and third). Irascible and domineering, a woman who atoned for earthly sins by giving the world a heavenly garden.

Then, after you've had your say, yea or nay, Mother Teresa or Lady Macbeth, you must ask yourself, what does it matter? The dear woman's ashes have been returned to the earth, in her own stupendous garden. The follies of the earth are temporal. The earth is eternal.

The dedication on her autobiography, *Always Room at the Top* reads:

> *Dedicated to*
> *all those who are seeking*
> *their place in the sun.*

All her life she sought her place in the sun. And with her garden at Lotusland, she found it.

(Right): Ganna Walska on her way to a party.
(Below Right): Ganna Walska hosting a garden tour of Lotusland in 1978.

THE HUSBANDS

"It is a well known fact that we are all born alone and we die alone. But with my inexhaustible capacity of feeling so much and so profoundly, I always live alone. Even when...two of us feel as one, nevertheless, ultimately we are alone, alone, always alone!! At least I always feel that I am alone. Alone..."
— Ganna Walska
— *Always Room at the Top*

And so she was. For though her marriages spanned twenty-eight years of elapsed time, Ganna Walska spent less than twenty percent of that time in common domicile with her mates.

Her autobiography, *Always Room at the Top*, contains thirty-seven pictures of her alone, eight pictures of her husbands alone, and no pictures of her with any of her husbands.

Through the kindness of time, the husbands of Madame Ganna Walska have become statistics. A book or more could easily be written about each one of them, as indeed was written about husband number six, Theos Bernard, by Madame Ganna Walska herself. It is titled *My Life With Yogi*, and is unpublished. Her first five husbands she deals with in her published, but out-of-print, book, *Always Room at the Top*. We have quoted her opinion of her husbands, none of whom could give us their opinion of her. We can, however, surmise from the letters from her husbands to her, now in the Lotusland archives, how much in love they seemed to be.

"A man in love is incomplete until he has married. Then he is finished."
—Zsa Zsa Gabor
Veteran of eight husbands

"When my faithful Mary brought the evening paper which related Madame Paderewski's death, I said:
'Mary, now I will marry Mr. Paderewski.'"
—Ganna Walska
—*Always Room at the Top*
(She didn't.)

"My husband, Mr. McCormick, he is different from Mr. Cochran. Mr. McCormick is all encouragement. No more will I get discourage (sic). I know Mr. McCormick believes in me and will help me to be successful.

Do I love Mr. McCormick? Most certainly that is no secret. We are in one thought. He is such a fine man. Such a big man. Whew!

This spring I go to Paris with my husband. I will have a season of opera at the Champs Elysées, which is now my own theatre, the gift of my husband. Next year I will return to America. Perhaps then I will appear in opera here...I want to convince the people of America that I can sing. That is my ambition. That is Mr. McCormick's ambition. How can I fail?"
—Interview attributed to Robert Murray

Madame Ganna Walska was a woman who couldn't bear to discard anything, whether a live plant or even a dead one (she had a driftwood garden for dead wood), or fifty-year-old correspondence. In one year, 1980, when she was ninety-three years old, she wrote eleven codicils to her 1979 will. In one of them, she directed her executors to call in her half-brother Eduarde to destroy all her personal papers. Later, she rescinded that codicil, but it seemed more to do with a disenchantment with her half-brother than a change of heart about the papers. A woman of ninety-three is entitled to forget a few things.

So, we have the benefit of her copious personal papers, and perhaps none are more poignant than the letters from her husbands. They attest to the powerful pull she had over the men she married. There are letters and telegrams from Dr. Fraenkel, Mr. Cochran, Mr. McCormick (beginning when she was married to Dr. Fraenkel) and Theos Bernard. The letters from Dr. Fraenkel are heartrending. About how he misses his "bebe", how his life is empty without her (she is in Havana, Cuba, singing with an opera company). He pleads with her to hurry home. He is in poor health and will die a year later.

McCormick's letters are more careful, but the longing for her shines through. There are loving references to their meetings, to how he certainly doesn't think she is toying with him to get on stage at his Chicago Opera Company, which for a time he virtually single-handedly kept afloat. He is as circumspect as you would imagine a gentleman who was still two husbands away from marrying her himself would be.

Theos Bernard's telegrams are full of declarations of love, and, as one might expect, natural and philosophical tidbits. He was, after all, he said, the only white lama.

Before her six husbands fade completely from her story, here are some statistics on them.

BARON ARCADIE D'EINGHORN

HUSBAND #1

OCCUPATION: Baron, Russian royalty.
HER AGE: 20
HIS AGE: approx. 25
ESTIMATED LENGTH OF COURTSHIP: Short—eloped.
MARRIAGE DATES: 1907 - 1915
BENEFITS TO BRIDE FROM MARRIAGE: Entrée to Russian royalty, wealth and prestige and social standing. Became a baroness. Rescued her from having to work for a living.
FINANCIAL SETTLEMENT: Unknown, but enough to send her independently on her way to Paris, then the U. S., and to keep up her singing lessons.
SYNOPSIS OF UNION: The baron spent the better part of the marriage and World War I in a tuberculosis sanitarium. Ganna Walska went to visit him three times, sometimes taking a room there. The baron was an incorrigible escapee from the sanitarium. Ganna Walska complained about his drinking and his irascible behavior (see also husband #5). The tubercular germs finally got him, but not before his bride got safely clear of him.
WALSKA'S VIEW: "He swore on his love for me he would die that instant if I did not forgive him. I was helpless...I could not complain to the doctors or he would no longer be allowed to stay in the sanitarium. I wanted to leave him.
  "He took out his revolver...
  "I stayed."

OCCUPATION: Doctor of neurology. Widely respected as physician of the rich and famous.
HER AGE: 29
HIS AGE: 49
ESTIMATED LENGTH OF COURTSHIP: Ten days. He proposed second office visit. Divorce from previous husband July 16, 1915. Marriage to Dr. Fraenkel, September 7, 1916.
MARRIAGE DATES: 1916 - 1920
BENEFITS TO BRIDE FROM MARRIAGE: U. S. citizenship. An adoring, wealthy, socially prominent American who kept the home fires burning while she trotted the hemisphere pursuing her "career."

HUSBAND #2

DOCTOR JOSEPH FRAENKEL

FINANCIAL SETTLEMENT: Inherited real estate and $500,000 cash after long battle with his family, who alleged fraud and undue influence. New York house sold for $116,000 in 1959.
SYNOPSIS OF UNION: She spoke of his wretched suffering from his final illness and claimed she didn't know he was ill when they married. She spent a large part of the short union away from home. He was also generous and indulgent, sending her many adoring letters as well as $1,500 to her in Cuba at Christmastime, 1918.
WALSKA'S VIEW: "When I married Dr. Fraenkel, I lost my personality..." "God had sent to earth a man with a soul great enough to heal human misery and then—without any apparent reason—took him away."

"Had God overdosed while making him too great?"

"Dr. Fraenkel's death was the end of everything that was and that could be. There was no God!"

> "The only color I see on the Heavens is you—I hope the sun shines upon you and for you—and you will bring some joy and happiness to me.
> With love!"
> —Letter from Dr. Joseph Fraenkel in New York to Ganna Walska in Havana, c. 1918

Dr. & Mrs. Joseph Fraenkel, New York City, 1919, one year before he died

OCCUPATION: Heir to carpet fortune. Yachtsman, polo player, playboy.
HER AGE: 33
HIS AGE: 46
ESTIMATED LENGTH OF COURTSHIP: He proposed on second sighting of her. Husband number four also interested, but still had a wife. Married less than five months after death of #2.
MARRIAGE DATES: 1920 - 1922: one year, eight months.
BENEFITS TO BRIDE FROM MARRIAGE: Married the richest bachelor in the world. He indulged her every whim: Rolls-Royce, Paris house, fur coat, jewelry, $100,000 a year spending money (about a million today).

HUSBAND #3

ALEXANDER SMITH COCHRAN

FINANCIAL SETTLEMENT: Twenty thousand dollars per year ($200,000 at today's dollar value), all personal property purchased during marriage. Home in Paris, rented for $7,000 per year, sold by Lotusland in 1988 for $2 million. She also got $3 million in his will ($30 million today). He died in 1931, the year husband number four, McCormick, divorced her for desertion.
SYNOPSIS OF UNION: Ganna Walska continued her quest for operatic fame and Mr. Cochran graciously sent her money on request to further that aim.

On her wedding night the bridegroom roamed the streets of Paris. The next day, while he was sleeping, Ganna entertained Mr. Harold McCormick (see husband #4), who was distraught Ganna had married so precipitously, without waiting for his divorce.

She was to leave on a ship for the United States days after the wedding. McCormick wanted to go with her. So did Cochran at the last minute, complicating matters. Ganna was to perform in an opera in McCormick's hometown of Chicago. Many glitches later, Ganna Walska walked out on the opera the day of the performance. She said it was to please her new husband and unrelated to any fear or temperament.

Mr. Cochran went to her hotel, only to find his wife was not registered as Mrs. Alexander Cochran, but Madame Ganna Walska, and he stormed out of town.

And it was all stormy from then on. In defense of her tenacious divorce-settlement demands, she claimed Alexander must be taught a lesson; that he could not treat women and wives as "things."
WALSKA'S VIEW: "After I married Mr. Cochran in Paris, I was much too preoccupied during the next two days helping Mr. McCormick to recover from the shock he received when he learned of the wedding, to indulge in any personal feelings."

"It was destiny that his laugh should exasperate me."

"A million francs worth of sable coat that I found in my room that afternoon, Alex's invitation to go with carte blanche to Cartier and choose anything I desired as a wedding present, and his businesslike announcement that my bank would receive a hundred thousand dollars yearly for my 'pin money'—all that went by me without actually touching my inner being."

> "What therefore God hath joined together, let not man put asunder."
> —Certificate of marriage of Alexander Smith Cochran and Ganna Walska

HUSBAND #4

OCCUPATION: Chairman of the board of the International Harvester Company.
HER AGE: 35   HIS AGE: 50
ESTIMATED LENGTH OF COURTSHIP: She met McCormick while she was married to Dr. Fraenkel. She instigated the meeting because he was a prime mover in the Chicago Opera Company, for which she had aspirations to sing. They exchanged many letters and met several times. When Dr. Fraenkel died, a courtship began, but within five months she had married Alex Cochran (see husband number three), not wishing to wait for Mr. McCormick's divorce. While she was married to Cochran, McCormick gave her her day in the sun with his Chicago Opera Company. This was her longest span between meeting and marriage, lasting through two previous husbands—probably about four years.
MARRIAGE DATES: 1922 - 1931

HAROLD McCORMICK

BENEFITS TO BRIDE FROM MARRIAGE: Entrée to the Chicago Opera Company. Mr. McCormick purchased for her the Théâtre des Champs Elysées, and a château in France, as well as the Chicago Light Opera House. During the marriage, he gave her over a million dollars (about ten million today).

During Ganna Walska's marriage to Cochran (#3), McCormick set up a trust fund for her, guaranteeing her $100,000 per year for life (one million today).
FINANCIAL SETTLEMENT: One hundred thousand dollars per year for life (one million today), the Paris theater (rent of $7,000 per year after '64—sold her interest in 1970 for $1,175,000).
SYNOPSIS OF UNION: Ganna Walska spent most of the marriage living apart from her husband. Just as she went to work at McCormick's Chicago Opera Company while married to Cochran, while married to McCormick she spent most of her marriage in France pursuing her operatic dream with the director of her theater, Walther Straram, who has been variously referred to as her mentor and close friend. Early in the marriage, Ganna Walska awoke in her château outside Paris to see on her estate every piece of farm machinery manufactured by McCormick's International Harvester Company. They were gifts from her distant husband.
WALSKA'S VIEW: "One of the most beautiful souls I have ever encountered in this valley of tears…was the delicately perfumed soul of Harold McCormick."

"Unfortunately that…idiosyncrasy led him to idolize the physical expression of love and he became insatiable in his search for the realization of the physical demands—insatiable because they were unobtainable for him any more. Nature, in her wisdom…had chosen for his second wife an idealist who was able to put so much value on the richness of his soul that she could not even imagine the possibility of his preferring to seek further for a gross and limited pleasure rather than being satisfied with the divine companionship of the spiritual love she was willing to share with him."

"Perhaps, I could have made Harold happy, but it would have been to the prejudice of my own soul's development which could accept only those sacrifices that pass through the fires of purification."

HUSBAND #5

OCCUPATION: Inventor of wireless telephone and weaponry.
HER AGE: 50
HIS AGE: 57
ESTIMATED LENGTH OF COURTSHIP: Five months.
MARRIAGE DATES: 1938-1941
BENEFITS TO BRIDE FROM MARRIAGE: Doing her share, she said, for the war effort by keeping up the spirits of this weapons inventor.
FINANCIAL SETTLEMENT: After his death (they had been separated for several years), Walska got a letter from Mr. Matthews' solicitor asking that she send £50 for funeral expenses. They had both executed prenuptial agreements forswearing any claim on the wealth of the other. Matthews was virtually a pauper.

HARRY GRINDELL-MATTHEWS

Mr. Grindell-Matthews to Marry Baroness
Owner of Champs Elysées Theatre
Romance of Science and Music

..."We met for the first time," he said, "at the Covent Garden opera three months ago... She has been coming over every weekend, because I am still at work. She is very sympathetic towards my endeavors and is anxious I should not lose any time in continuing my work until it is completed..."

The baroness left Paris...by train or aeroplane, and was on the way to some destination which Mr. Grindell-Matthews could not name...

Mr. Grindell-Matthews, who at one time was called "Death-Ray Matthews," a soubriquet, by the way, of which he is tired has become famous for his experiments with light rays.

He was the first to make moving pictures and record sound simultaneously, but his most notable invention was radio-telephony.
—*From an interview with Grindell-Matthews in The Western Mail, Cardiff, Wales, August, 1937*

SYNOPSIS OF UNION: She was listed as a baroness in wedding announcements in English newspapers. Disillusioned early on, the couple separated less than a year after the marriage.

WALSKA'S VIEW: "Could it be...that science changed the substance of his soul into self-accommodating clay?"

"He was always suing someone for calumny. He always defended his good name through the offices of his solicitor...."

"Everything about him was negative. He looked older than his age. He seemed haggard. Quite blind in one eye, his other saw but little. His hands trembled so he could hardly lift his glass of vermouth to his lips from which a cigarette eternally dangled."

"Must I be as little as a *wife* in order to become bigger?"

"...I understand from mutual friends that he is a very charming personality and a gentleman. But Ganna, he is an inventor. All inventors are temperamental and 'cracked-pots' in one way or another, otherwise they would not possess the genius necessary to invent things. This is not intended as criticism of Mr. Matthews—on the contrary, it is a compliment when I call him a genius.

"But the point of this letter is that you are temperamental yourself and given to wild rages and varying moods. Both you and Mr. Matthews must have a tremendous amount of courage to think that two temperamental artists will get along like two bugs in a rug."
—*Letter from Ganna Walska's attorney, Phelan Beale, September, 1937, two weeks after engagement was announced*

HUSBAND #6

OCCUPATION: "White Lama," Ph.D. student, yogi, former lawyer.
HER AGE: 55
HIS AGE: 32
ESTIMATED LENGTH OF COURTSHIP: He proposed on the second sighting of her. (see husband #3). She said it was a ridiculous notion.
MARRIAGE DATES: 1942 - 1946
BENEFITS TO BRIDE FROM MARRIAGE: Interest in Eastern religions had been growing in this Roman Catholic heart, and the White Lama embodied a quest for spirituality that she shared. She said he made her feel good about her body for the first time. He found the Lotusland property for her and persisted until she bought it.

Theos Bernard at Tibetland (Lotusland)

THEOS BERNARD

Inscribed, "To Ganna—May the blessings of love always be yours. Theos—1940"

FINANCIAL SETTLEMENT: She paid him $1,500 to vacate the "Penthouse of the Gods" she had purchased for him in the mountains so he could meditate at a higher altitude, and paid $5,000 for his attorney's fees. He had asked the court for alimony payments, claiming she had spoiled him with her wealth, but they, too, had signed prenuptial agreements relinquishing all rights and claims to the wealth and property of the other.

SYNOPSIS OF UNION: She spent the better part of each year in New York attending the Metropolitan Opera (where she appeared once in a bare-midriff dress and fur coat), while Theos studied for his Ph.D. (which he received during the marriage).

She couldn't pronounce Theos Bernard's first name, she said, because it was God, and so pretentious.

Ganna Walska claimed he was unreasonably demanding of her.

WALSKA'S VIEW: "So considering the gravity of our situation that jeopardized the salvation of his soul when I became a widow, I decided in spite of great personal unwillingness, to marry him in order that he may have the security of mind for which he craved so much."

"They (the divorce lawyers) simply could not allow themselves to believe…that I never was in love with Dr. Bernard. Dealing with the application of an inflexible black on white law, they excluded a possibility of abstract selflessness."

"They looked at this intimate extremely subtle drama of two old souls as any common case of a rich and mature woman marrying a young and poor man who professed to be a writer but who actually was living on women's credulity and their money in exchange for some dubious yoga's exercises such as standing on the head per example."

Many people who become avid collectors, whether of Tiffany lamps or palm trees, Jim Beam Whiskey bottles or fountain pens, liken their zest for collecting to a disease. They, for the most part, are helpless to explain the strange malady that grips them like a rampant fever when they are exposed to the beloved objects of their desire.

(Right): Madame Ganna Walska participating in the theater.
(Below): Ganna Walska as "Queen Barbara of Poland", entering the Grand Prix Ball in Paris, c. 1924.

WALSKA'S INTERESTS

Madame Ganna Walska must have experienced this countless times throughout her active collecting lifetime. Fortunately, she was in the enviable position of one who never need turn her back on her heart's delight for lack of sufficient funds. As a result, she collected lustily, and when she was finally finished with her quests, the results were astonishing. She truly was, as she said, "the enemy of the average."

Her first and earliest love was, of course, the opera stage.

Walska's adoration of clothes and jewelry are legend. She was always the one at the party with the most flamboyant hat, the greatest lump of gemstone, the most startling dress. None of her stuff was off the rack. *She* wasn't off the rack, why should her apparel be?

> "Because I am not dressed as Number 2768 of Schiaparelli, Mainbocher's 'Wally Blue' or Molyneux's Spring Model 1938, people may call me eccentric when I am only original in the true meaning of the word."
> — *Ganna Walska*

Madame Walska launched a perfume business with a fanfare that would make a press agent blush. She dressed in her most elaborate wardrobe, adorned with her most expensive jewels, and trotted out the Rolls. And as usual, she was talked about more than the product, though she must have realized, in a large measure she *was* the product. The business floundered, but the jewels increased in value. She also announced she was going to open a beauty shop, but didn't.

When the aristocratic expatriates left Russia with their heirlooms, Ganna Walska was in Paris, dressed as a peasant, to greet them—to turn their treasures into hard currency. Some called her a wise businesswoman, others an opportunist. So much is in the eye of the beholder.

(Right): Madame Ganna Walska launches her perfume venture.

"The Garden is my Résumé"

Drawing by Victoria Roberts, © 1994 The New Yorker Magazine, Inc.

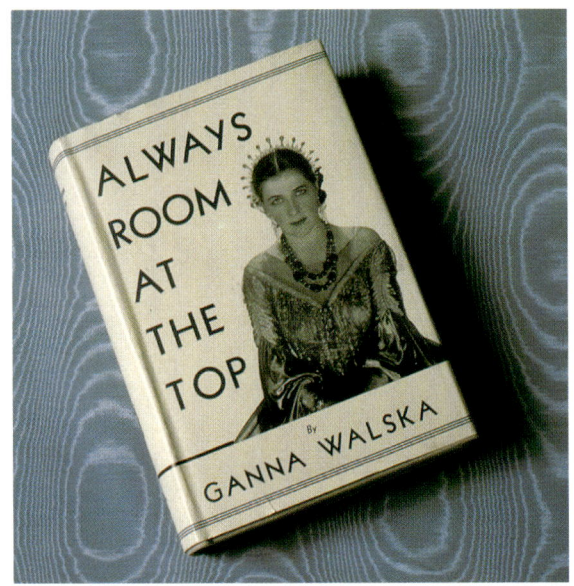

(Left): Ganna Walska's autobiography
(Above): A selection of her carousel horse collection
(Right): Madame Walska in her backyard with one of her bird cages, 1958.

(Below): Costume for Madame for Madame Butterfly

(Below): One example of Walska's astonishing jewelry collection

She collected autographed pictures of celebrities, attesting to their friendship. Among her collection are Toscanini (2), Debussy, Caruso, Richard Strauss, Leopold Stokowski, Fritz Kreisler, Lauritz Melchior, Pope Pius XI, Franklin Roosevelt and Mussolini.

Ganna Walska wrote two books; one published, one not. She underwrote other publications (Theos Bernard wrote a book dedicated to her, published four years after their divorce) and funded musical performances.

She collected carousel horses for a while, Tibetan art in another period (she willed the eight-hundred-piece collection to a Buddhist sect in Colorado), dresses, hats, jewelry, shoes, cars, then birds. These interests were not taken lightly, but were all pursued with her patented passion. When she died there were seven cars in her garage. Thousands of items of wearing apparel were given to the Los Angeles County Museum of Art by Madame Walska's niece Hania Puacz Tallmadge, an heir to the Puascz beauty.

Madame Walska was a magnetic, exuberant woman whose appetites were not retiring.

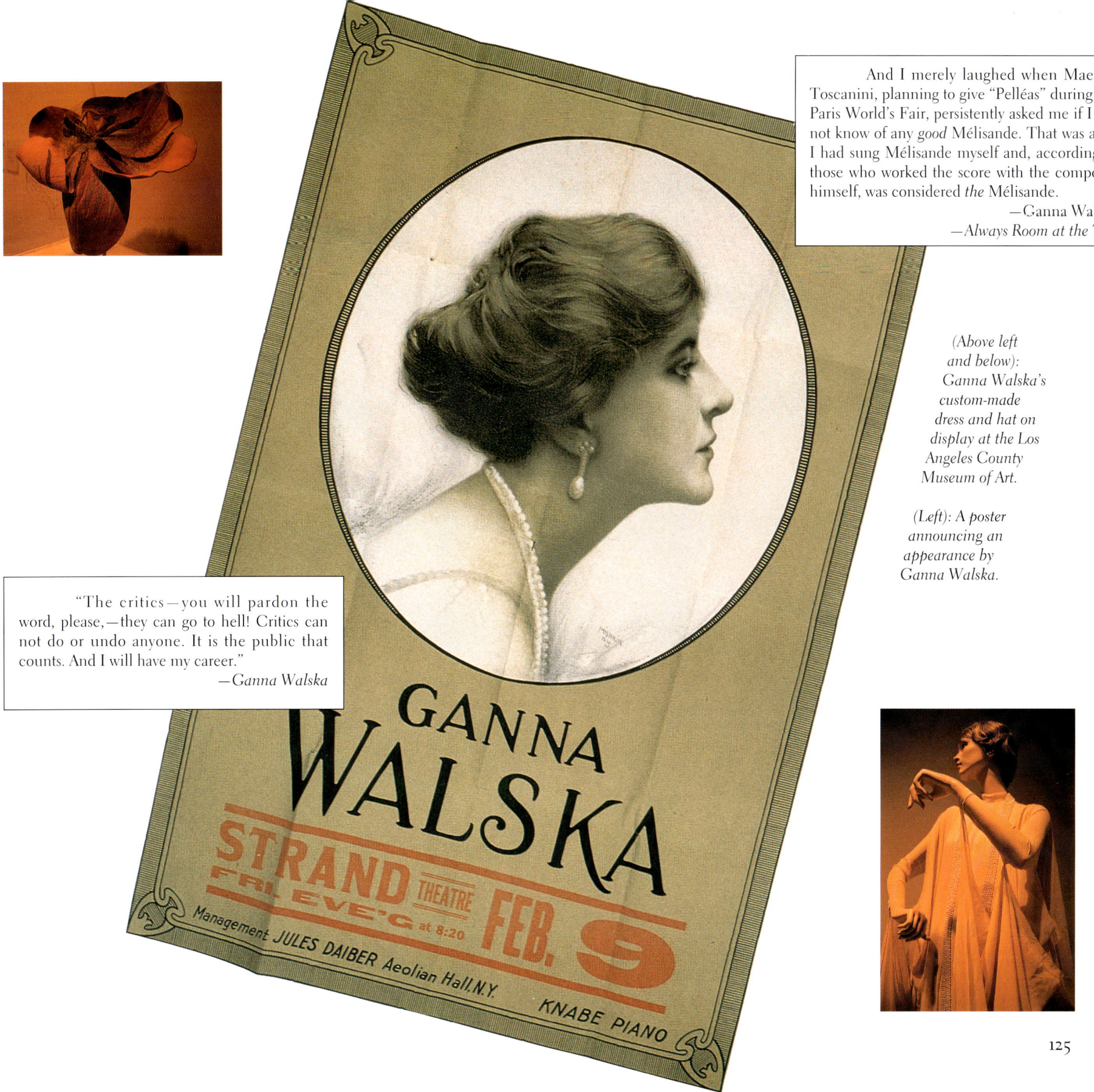

And I merely laughed when Maestro Toscanini, planning to give "Pelléas" during the Paris World's Fair, persistently asked me if I did not know of any *good* Mélisande. That was after I had sung Mélisande myself and, according to those who worked the score with the composer himself, was considered *the* Mélisande.
—Ganna Walska
—*Always Room at the Top*

(Above left and below): Ganna Walska's custom-made dress and hat on display at the Los Angeles County Museum of Art.

(Left): A poster announcing an appearance by Ganna Walska.

"The critics—you will pardon the word, please,—they can go to hell! Critics can not do or undo anyone. It is the public that counts. And I will have my career."
—Ganna Walska

127

GANNA WALSKA BUILDS HER GARDEN 1941-1984

"If my innocent ambition in attempting to raise the consciousness of the world's most illustrious inhabitants who crossed my path, those who direct the moral pulse of the universe — if that ambition can somehow mark my passage here below, because I lighted in those people the creative spark so essential to the chosen, so indispensable to the apostleship of a life dedicated like mine to inner beauty profoundly implanted in the soul — if I have been allowed to be an inspiration to few or even to one, I will be satisfied. Confucius said: 'He who planted a tree did not pass on this earth in vain.'"

—Ganna Walska, *Always Room at the Top*

Out front, the tasteful letters on the gatepost say simply:

GANNA WALSKA
LOTUSLAND

It was, like everything else in the garden, her own decision. It is an interesting selection, especially in light of all the other possibilities, like Ganna Walska's Lotusland, Lotusland of Ganna Walska, Lotusland with Ganna Walska underneath, or just plain Lotusland.

Why did she select the appellation she did for her pride and joy, the culmination of her struggle to make a difference?

We must understand the pieces of her life, to better understand the whole.

Her life changed dramatically after she was free of her last husband. There are more and broader smiles on the pictures of the middle-aged and older woman than there are on those of the young beauty.

It is as though she thought beauty must be taken seriously, lest anyone suspect the beauty frivolous.

Two sisters, both over one hundred years old, were photographed for the *Smithsonian* magazine. They were asked the secret of their longevity. The youngest replied, "Honey, we never did have husbands to worry us to death."

Ganna Walska was no longer worried. It was as though the burden had been lifted. Perhaps it was just the mellowing of age, perhaps it was the flight of her albatross when she finally admitted she would not have an opera career. And, more probably, it was the fascination she had for the garden and the magnetic pull her garden had for her.

Ironically, it is the sixth and final husband to whom we owe the gratitude for finding, selecting and encouraging (not to say nagging) her to buy the property that is now Lotusland.

Then there was the matter of the money; she had stored up quite a lot of it and Ganna Walska was not one to let resources sit idly by. She was financially secure and was more at peace with herself than ever before.

And refurbishing twenty-five acres of thirty-seven would not come cheaply, especially not the way Ganna Walska went about things.

She started at the house and once that was completed she fanned out to the other areas until finally she came to rest in the peerless cycad garden bordering Sycamore Canyon Road. This she claimed to have financed by a second sale of jewelry, which netted her almost one million dollars. But by then, that was a small portion of her wealth.

Fortunately, she was allotted sufficient time on this earth to complete her dream. Ninety-seven years, by the best count, forty-three of them at work on her garden.

Everyone who worked for Madame Ganna Walska had a favorite story to tell. Most of them with affection: "I loved her" crept into a lot of the tellings of "My Life

(Left): Cycad Garden under construction, 1978

with Madame." The narratives were not unrelieved sweetness and light—the great lady apparently had her moods, her flashes of impatience, of irrationality, of irresolution, of impetuosity and even of imperialism. But these momentary lapses were as quickly covered with kindness and cookies and the passing out of gratifying bonuses.

By all accounts, she was an extremely generous employer. Her gardeners got not only $1000 Christmas bonuses, they got bonuses at Easter, the fourth of July and Labor Day. Most of the gardeners at Lotusland received $20,000 from her in her will. There were over thirty personal bequests in that document, the final one drawn in 1979 and amended fourteen more times before she died in early 1984.

She was also reportedly extremely difficult to work for. Demanding, yes, but erratic and irascible—unpredictable, frustrating, suffocating even. It sometimes seemed she had her heart set on emasculating men—but the few women under her control fared no better. One day she called you a genius, the next a fool. She tried to find someone to follow in her footsteps and had several false starts with short-lived directors until she settled on Charles Glass, who did remarkable work for Lotusland for twelve years.

But from his intelligent account of his years at Lotusland, it was far from easy. Mr. Glass tells engaging stories of his meetings with Ganna Walska. She would speak nonstop, and if he tried to talk she would cut him off with, "Pul leese, I am talking. When I finish you may talk." But she would continue unabated until she finally said, "Now I am too tired to continue, I must rest."

(Above): Cacti and Bromeliads with bathhouse in distance

To get his points to her, Charles Glass wrote her long letters. They are in the Lotusland archives, with great blue circles around words and red underscores under phrases, paragraphs slashed and an occasional terse comment in the margins. Even in the solitude of her room, reading his letters, she was combative.

He claims he told her the reason her English was not stronger was that she heard so little of it; she was talking all the time. But he loved the work and felt privileged to work for someone for whom money was no object. The constant conflicts with the controlling Madame got him down. But Glass admits that when Madame Ganna Walska was finally bedridden and out of the fray, he missed her and he found his job "stultifyingly boring."

Madame Ganna Walska's life was the opera, and her relentless pursuit to perform it. She practiced it, longed to perform it and attended it with an awesome faithfulness. When she came to build her garden, the opera that was in her became part of the garden.

She began her forty-three-year project in 1941, at the house. There were some cacti around the main structure and the famous landscape architect Lockwood de Forest wrote to her in that year, suggesting she consider more cacti at the entry. A year later he was applauding her genius for her cactus plantings.

Planting the twenty-five acre garden was a lifetime undertaking, and Ganna Walska poured her passion into it every step. It was her vision and personality, her charm and virtuosity that put their stamp on her grand garden. It was the product of a soul driven to achieve something great.

Gardens are always personal creations, like any work of art. No two can be alike, because no two people have the same fingerprints. And no garden is more personal than Ganna Walska Lotusland.

Gardens change every day. Kinton Stevens gave it some trees which are now, one hundred-plus years later, magnificent specimens. Ganna Walska's contributions began over fifty years ago, and her operatic massings of plants give it its own patina of beauty and drama. In time Kinton Stevens's plantings will be gone—plants may often live longer than people, but they don't live forever. The Chilean wine palms (*Jubaea chilensis*) are showing some signs of old age. Everything passes.

The landscaper's art is a fluid art. Every day the plants' relationships to one another changes. They grow at different rates, some die. Often they do the unexpected. It is part of the beauty of a garden that it has these endless variations on the same theme. In time Ganna Walska's garden will take on a life of its own. Her creation has already passed to other hands, and other influences will be felt. Plants will die because they have outlived their natural

(Left): Massed Bromeliads in lower Bromeliad garden

(Below): Ganna Walska picking her flowers, 1958.

(Above): Ganna Walska being driven by her faithful chauffeur, Walter, c. 1970.

cycle, just as she did. Perhaps that was part of her rationale of the mass plantings—strength in numbers.

In her garden, Madame Ganna Walska wore the same floppy hat for forty years, she had favorite tattered clothing. Gone were the spectacular jewels and the startling dresses and custom-made hats. She had retuned to nature and was more at home in her garden than on any other opera stage, and the smiles of childhood had returned to her face.

Every day she was in her garden, and every day they became more vast and complex. She went with relish on plant-collecting safaris, buying with a spirited appetite that seemed never sufficiently fed.

She attended plant-society meetings and plant sales, scoured nurseries, corresponded with specialty plantsmen who brought her plants from the wild. She shopped for statues, bricks, tile, slag, abalone shells. She climbed mountains to select just the right rocks. Then saw to it they were put in just the right place, because nobody else could have her vision. Nobody else had lived her life, nobody else had the links of her genetic chain.

She was hostess to the Cactus and Succulent Society, the Palm Society, the Bromeliad Society, the Fern Society and dozens of other worthy groups. For each she planned her functions with meticulous care and brought them off with a panache that only she could.

Often before these events she was driven to beef up her collections to show how artfully spectacular these forlorn plants could look in large groupings.

(Above): Epiphyllum *on carved totem, 1978*
(Below Right): A young Lotusland visitor enjoys the concrete statues.

And she wanted no signs on the plants, telling what they were. In fact, she didn't know what they were called. That was not what she was about. That was the science of botany, and she was an artist. A poet of plants. It didn't matter to her what some taxonomist decided to *call* a plant, what mattered to her was what it looked like.

> Garden is more beautiful than ever, did tremendous things this summer, two extraordinary rock gardens and thousand more cactuses, this time already from Arizona and Texas and they are segregated, every kind separately...
> —From letter, Ganna Walska to Irma and Christian Rub, October 22, 1948

In her garden she was the impresario, the music director, the stage manager, art director, makeup artist and lighting technician. She had a stellar cast of landscape architects, designers, masonry contractors, tile setters and gardeners, but it was her production, beginning to end. She coaxed and cajoled, sweet-talked, encouraged, punished, rewarded, tricked and dictated them all into action. She was a stern taskmistress with a new, generous smile that flashed in appreciation as her masterwork took shape.

Ganna Walska had no children, but plants can be like children: they have a life cycle and respond to nourishment. Some think they respond to verbal encouragement. She did, and she talked to her plants as she watched the children of her garden grow. She wasn't too keen on the baby stage and usually adopted them older.

(Above): Lone cactus flower in gravel, 1977
(Left): Bromeliads, 1977
(Below): Lotus in Japanese Garden pond, 1977

My home in Santa Barbara is known as Lotusland. During the last 25 or more years I have greatly expanded the 40 acres of this property, devoting myself exclusively to establish and increase constantly already respectfully valuable collection with great variety of species such as Palms, Cycads, etc., from all around the world in picturesque display and setting, landscaping each variety in separate bed more suitable for semi-tropical plants to adapt themselves in our California beautiful climate being equal to their native environment. Time and circumstances permitting, I hopefully dreamt that if given all the opportunities having considerable finances at my disposal I might fulfill my work to develop Lotusland to its maximum capacity into the most outstanding center of horticultural significance and of educational use.
—*From the Last Will & Testament of Ganna Walska, 1979*

Her garden is as dramatic as she was. It has her music and her spectacle. Lotusland is what it is because she made it so. It was not an endeavor that came cheaply. Many millions of dollars went into the showplace.

Numerous people aspire to build gardens, often in their later years. There may be a quest for immortality in planting things that will live beyond us. Many people succeed with small gardens, some fewer with larger ones. Government entities are often able to take a private garden and expand it or even create one from the dust of the ground. But individuals who can command the resources and offer the talent over forty years to create a garden the size and scope of Lotusland are almost unheard of today.

But Ganna Walska was not a woman who could sit still amid a treasure-trove of gold, silver and diamonds. She had to be doing something to fulfill her destiny. Jewels and furs and Rolls-Royces were in her past, and she no longer spoke of her past. Her old life was the overture to her opera which is now being performed daily at Lotusland.

And her opera is everywhere you look. Walking through dark corridors, you are thrust upon a theater and stage setting of stunning beauty in each of the gardens. And each is as distinct from another as is one opera from another.

And so, perhaps the solution to the riddle of the elegant lettering on the entry-gate post:

It is the long-sought billing of Madame of her name over the title of an opera. Like:

Mary Garden
Pelléas et Mélisande

Amelita Galli-Curci
La Traviata

Leontyne Price
Aïda

And now, finally:

GANNA WALSKA
LOTUSLAND

(Above): The entry-gate post for Ganna Walska Lotusland
(Left): Path to tall Dioon spinulosum *cycad*

ADDITIONAL PHOTO CAPTIONS

Key		
T = top	TL = top left	TC = top center
TR =top right	C =center	CL = center left
CM =center middle		CR = center right
B = bottom		BL = bottom left
BC = bottom center		BR = bottom right

Pages:
Front cover: giant *Tridacna* clam shells in aloe garden with *Aloe striata*, 1979
1: View through window from inside house of *Euphorbia ingens* (tall) and *Echinocactus grusonii* (Golden barrel cactus) on ground.
2: *Victoria regia cv. Longwood*
3: water gardens with *Jubaea chilensis* (Chilean wine palm), *Podocarpus elatus* reflected in pond, Papyrus on right, 1990
4: *Nelumbo nucifera* (Lotus)
5: water gardens and view of bathhouse (designed by George Washington Smith), in 1989
6: aloe pond with abalone shells
7: Tree aloes rise above the aloe garden in the fog, 1980.
8-9: the three stars of the cycad garden, *Encephalartos woodii*, over pond
10: Sycamore Canyon main gate with *Agave franzosinii*, 1980
11T: *Nelumbo nucifera* (Lotus)
11B: first Lotusland Sign, c. 1946
12: various bromeliads under *Quercus agrifolia* with cactus, in the background, 1990
13: tortured *Euphorbia ingens* in front of main house, 1990
14: view of cycad garden, 1987
15: *Nelumbo nucifera* (Lotus)
22TC: *Nelumbo nucifera* (Lotus) and *Nelumbo cultivar*
22BL: *Bowiea volubilis* (Climbing onion) from South Africa
22CL: a well with aloe hybrids in the background, 1978
22BR: *Aloe candelabrum* foreground, *Aloe marlothii*, background, 1979
23: Bromeliads (mid-ground, Varigated pineapple) and cacti; some *Cephalocereus senilis* (Old man cactus)
24-25: tall *Euphorbia ingens* against house, *Echinocactus grusonii* (Golden barrel cactus) on ground, tall palm in background is *Washingtonia filifera* hybrid

25R: *Euphorbia ingens, Echinocactus grusonii* (Golden barrel cactus) *and Neobuxbaumia polylopha* (on right, flanking walkway to house)
26TL: main house wall with *Euphorbia ingens*
26TR: main house from below: architectural detail
26BL: the pavilion surrounded by cacti; *Tricocereus*, right foreground
26BR: Bromeliads in bloom under *Quercus agrifolia*
27: rose garden, 1977
29TL: lawn with *Cymbidium* under *Quercus agrifolia*, whaling pot at right foreground with *Cymbidium*, 1979
29BL: gate to pavilion, c. 1977
29TR: tile fountain at the new visitor center
29BR: lawn with *Cymbidium*, with whaling pot, 1979
30-31: concrete statues from Ganna Walska's country home outside of Paris
32TL: cacti, bromeliads, (*Neoregelia* and Varigated pineapple), and agaves, 1990
32TR: neptune fountain and rear view of main house, 1989
32BC: old walnut orchard in spring, 1982
33TL: lawn toward rear of house; palm frond is *Phoenix reclinata*, 1979
33C: rear view of house, 1977
33BL: back patio and rose garden, now called the parterre
34TL: concrete statuary with Jade plant at left
34TC: *Stenocereus marginatus*
34TR: *Notocactus leninghausii*
34B: *Notocactus leninghausii* foreground, *Cephalocereus senilis* (Old man cactus) in background with the pavilion
35TL: *Cephalocereus senilis* (Old man cactus), foreground *Mammillaria*, 1978
35TC: view of front entry from inside main house
35TR: *Kalanchoe beharensis* and concrete statues, 1977
35B: the southern end of the cactus garden, large cactus is *Myrtillocactus geometrizans*, tall cactus on right is *Pilosocereus*, with the blue garden in background, 1990
36L: *Echinocactus grusonii* (Golden barrel cactus) and *Cephalocereus senilis* (Old man cactus)
36C: *Cephalocereus senilis* (Old man cactus) and *Notocactus leninghausii*, outside pavilion
36R: old crested cacti grafts

37: *Notocactus leninghausii*
38L: *Neobuxbaumia polylopha*, foreground, *Euphorbia ingens*, background right
38R: *Cephalocereus senilis* (Old man cactus), 1977
39L: night-blooming *Cereus* and *Tricocereus* on right, 1977
39R: *Euphorbia ingens* shadowed on house
40-41: *Euphorbias* near the house, foreground left is *Euphorbia horrida*, tallest is *Euphorbia obovalifolia*, 1990
42L: Foreground is *Puya laxa*, on rock is *Echeveria*, background is *Kalanchoe fedtschenkoi* (purple scallops)
42R: *Echeveria*
43: *Aeonium arboreum atropurpureum* "Zwartkop", 1978
44: *Aloe mitriformis* with coral, 1977
45L: *Echinocactus grusonii* (Golden barrel cactus) and pavilion in background
45R: *Echinocactus grusonii* (Golden barrel cactus)
46L: *Dracaena draco* (Dragon tree)
46R: *Euphorbia resinifera*, foreground and *Euphorbia obovalifolia*, 1990
47: *Trichocereus terscheckii* in moonlight, 1994
48: *Woodwardia fimbriata* (Giant chain fern), 1977
49: the fern garden with Staghorn ferns in tree, 1977
50: *Sphaeropteris cooperi* (Australian treefern), 1979
51: view of the fern garden, 1987
52: left with white flowers, *Brugmansia*; *Sphaeropteris cooperi* (Australian treefern) foreground, 1990
53: Staghorn fern, *Platycerium bifurcatum* on tree, 1990
54TL: the aloe garden with a hybrid in the background, *Aloe arborescens* X *ferox* (*Aloe salm-dyckiana*)
54TR: aloe pond, 1977
54BL: *Aloe candelabrum*
54BR: foreground is *Aloe spectabilis*, Aloe hybrids in background
55: *Aloe bainesii*
56L: *Aloe marlothii*
56-57: the aloe pond, with giant *Tridacna* clam shells, abalone shells, aloes and palms; *Aloe ramosissima* on right behind fountain, 1990
58: *Aloe candelabrum*
59TL: *Aloe plicatilis* foreground, trunk of *Beaucarnea stricta* left; back right, *Phoenix reclinata*, 1990

59BR: one of the footpaths in the aloe garden, 1990
60TL: foreground is *Aloe spectabilis*, middle ground right is hybrid *Aloe arborescens X ferox* (*Aloe salm-dyckiana*), tree in background is *Aloe bainesii*
60CR: *Aloe marlothii*
60BL: left foreground is *Aloe candelabrum*, right is *Aloe spectabilis*, *Jubaea chilensis* (Chilean wine palms) in background
61CL: the aloe garden
61TR: the aloe garden, tall aloe blooming in back is *Aloe ferox*
61BR: *Aloe candelabrum*
62TL: *Aloe bainesii* (right), *Aloe dichotoma* on left
62B: giant *Tridacna* clam shells with *Aloe striata*, 1979
63: *Aloe mutabilis* in foreground, *Aloe spectabilis* blooming and Aloe hybrids in back with *Butia* palms, 1979
64TL: blooming on left is *Aloe mutabilis*, tall aloe is *Aloe marlothii*, lower bushes are *Aloe spectabilis*, other blooming are hybrids (*Aloe salm-dyckiana*)
64BR: foreground is *Aloe plicatilis*, *Aloe spinosissima* on right, large blooming *Aloe ferox* in background, and other Aloe hybrids
65: foreground is *Aloe spinosissima*, left is *Aloe mutabilis*, also *Aloe arborescens X humilis*
66: on left is *Aloe arborescens*, tree aloe is *Aloe excelsa*, right foreground is *Aloe succotrina*, rear right are Aloe hybrids
67: aloes in the fog: *Aloe bainesii* on right, palm on left is *Jubaea chilensis* (Chilean wine palm), 1977
68T: portrait of Ganna Walska by Coles Phillips
68B: blue hue in the succulent garden with *Pachypodium lamierei* on left, *Calabanis hookeri* on right
69: *Brahea armata* (Blue hesper palm), 1990
70TL: *Calabanis hookeri* and *Echeveria*
70BR: *Brahea armata* (Blue hesper palm) below and *cedrus atlantic v. glauca* (Atlas cedar) above right
71T: with blue-green slag from a bottling company bordering walk, tall thorny plants left background, *Pachypodium lamierei*, left foreground around rock *Aeonium arboreum atropurpureum* "Zwartkop", *Echeveria* and *Calabanis hookeri* in back
71B: *Cedrus atlantica v. glauca* (Atlas cedar) and *Agave franzonsinii*
71C: three sizes of *Brahea armata* (Blue hesper palm)
72T: Japanese pond with cranes, 1978
72BL: *Nelumbo nucifera* (Lotus)
72R-73L: Japanese pond shoreline, 1982
74L: *Acer palmatum atropurpureum* (Japanese maple)
74R: Japanese pond in moonlight, 1994
75: Lotus through Torii gate in the Japanese Garden, 1977
76: Swans on Japanese pond, 1983
77: Japanese pond with lotus; *Cycas revoluta* (Sago palm) on left
78: *Nelumbo nucifera* (Lotus)

79: Japanese pond with live egret, 1991
80: TC—tile benches at water garden
    All other 80: *Nelumbo nucifera* (Lotus)
81L: *Eichhornia crassipes* (Water hyacinth) in water stairs, 1977
81R: water garden with water lilies and bathhouse, 1989
82: *Nelumbo nucifera* (Lotus)
83: *Nelumbo nucifera* (Lotus) except 83CL and 83TR
    83CL: *Nelumbo* cultivars
    83TR: *Agapanthus orientalis* background, *Nelumbo nucifera* (Lotus) foreground
84L: *Nelumbo nucifera* (Lotus)
84R: night-blooming tropical water lily
85L: *Victoria regia* cv. Longwood hybrid
85R: water spouting from water garden (former pool) with fish statue in foreground, 1979
86TL: water garden with Papyrus rising, water lilies in foreground, 1978
86TR: hardy water lilies
86BL: *Nelumbo nucifera* (Lotus)
86BR: *Nelumbo nucifera* (Lotus)
87: water garden with *Nelumbo* in foreground, 1990
88-89: *Nelumbo nucifera* (Lotus) except
    88CR: *Nelumbo lutea*
    88CM: hardy water lily
    89CL: *Nelumbo* cultivar
90: Palm vista from main-residence courtyard, left to right *Phoenix canariensis*, *Washingtonia filfera* hybrid and *Syagrus romanzoffiana*
91T: *Howea forsteriana* (Kentia palms)
91B: *Brahea edulis*
92TL: *Jubaea chilensis* (Chilean wine palms)
92TR: *Jubaea chilensis* (Chilean wine palms), *Brahea armata* (Blue hesper palm) beneath, *Furcraea roezlii* on ground, middle
92C: *Brahea armata* (Blue hesper palm)
92BL: *Rhyopalostylis sapida*, background
92BR: *Livistona chinensis*, center; *Jubaea chilensis* (Chilean wine palms), background
93: *Jubaea chilensis* (Chilean wine palms) with *Dracaena draco* (Dragon trees) below
94TL: *Phoenix reclinata*, tall left, right *Howea forsteriana* (Kentia palm), 1990
94TR: *Jubaea chilensis* (Chilean wine palms) in aloe garden
94BL: *Butia* leaves and seeds
94BR: *Howea forsteriana* (Kentia palm), 1990
95: back of house, yard, *Phoenix reclinata* on left, large Monterey cypress (*Cupressus macrocarpa*) on right
96TL: female cone of *Encephalartos arenarius*
96TR: view of the cycad garden, 1987
96B: view of the cycad garden
97: cycad garden foreground, right is *Encephalartos altensteinii*, 1990

98: view of the cycad garden, 1987
99: *Encephalartos* in background, *Dioon* in foreground with metate (stone), in the old cycad garden (now the shade palm garden), 1977
100TL: *Dioon spinulosum*
100BR: *Lepidozamia peroffskyana*, 1979
101: standing on top of hill in cycad garden, *Dioon* in background overlook *Encephalartos* in foreground, 1987
102TL: *Encephalartos woodii*, 1980
102TR: three different species of *Encephalartos*: *Encephalartos friderici-guilielmi* on left, *Encephalartos transvenosus* on right, *Encephalartos lehmannii* center background
102BL: different species of *Encephalartos*, 1987
102BR: group of *Dioon*, 1993
103: *Lepidozamia peroffskyana*
104T: *Encephalartos paucidentatus* with *Encephalartos pteregonus* in right background
104B: view of cycad garden with *Encephalartos*, 1990
105: *Macrozamia* and *Ceratozamia* in the old cycad garden, (now the shade palm garden), 1977
106: the young Ganna Walska
112: from left to right: Baron Arcadie d'Einghorn, Dr. Joseph Fraenkel, Alexander Smith Cochran, Harold McCormick, Harry Grindell-Matthews, Theos Bernard
119: Buddha statue with lotus blossom, 1977
120TL: a stand of *Howea forsteriana* (Kentia palms)
120-121: cycad garden: *Encephalartos lehmannii*, 1990
121R: *Nelumbo nucifera* (Lotus)
126TL: Bromeliads, 1990
126BR: *Aloe bainesii* in front of *Jubaea chilensis* (Chilean wine palms)
127TL: *Sedum morganianum* (Burro-tail) on oak tree in moonlight, lawn area; the "hats" protect the plants from the birds, 1994.
127BL: close up detail of *Aloe spinosissima*
127TR: lawn area and hanging *Sedum morganianum* (Burro-tail) in fog, *Agave franzosinii* right foreground, 16th century globes in front, 1978
127BR: *Epicactus* species, now part of succulent garden, 1978
128: Ganna Walska in front of main house, *Cereus peruvianus* in foreground, *Echinocactus grusonii* (Golden barrel cactus) middle, *Euphorbia ingens* left, 1958
129: Lotusland spelled out in succulents at the Sycamore Canyon gate, c. 1950.
136TL: *Nelumbo nucifera* (Lotus)
136CL: *Nelumbo nucifera* (Lotus)
136BL: *Nelumbo nucifera* (Lotus)
136-137: Aloe pond with *Aloe speciosa* (tree aloes) on right, and *Aloe plicatilis* (bush aloes), 1990
142: view of property from south, now Lotusland, c. 1880s
143: view of the bathhouse and water gardens, c. 1950
144: Ganna Walska at Lotusland, 1980
Back cover: individual *Nelumbo nucifera* (Lotus)

Wm. B. Dewey has been photographing the landscape of Southern California since 1970. A native of San Diego, he attended UC Davis, Rochester Institute of Technology, and Brooks Institute of Photography. Dewey's private pilot license enables him to capture striking aerial photographs of the landscape, some of which were featured in *Santa Barbara Magazine*. His aerial video footage of Baja California was used in the BBC and PBS documentary, *The Mystery of Laguna Baja*. Dewey also photographs for many Santa Barbara and Santa Cruz Island organizations, including the Lotusland Foundation.

Gregory L. Padgett came to Santa Barbara from Michigan in 1972. While pursuing a life in the arts (watercolors, landscape design, textiles), an interest in photography developed with the focus on the gardens and architecture of gated estates. Over a 20-year period, his collection has become recognized as one of the most important historical and artistic photographic records of Montecito. Because of his long personal relationship with Madame Ganna Walska, Padgett was given unusual access to the gardens in her lifetime. He took hundreds of rare photographs of Lotusland in this unique developmental stage.

Artist and Author, **Robert Glenn Ketchum's** photographic print work is represented in most of the major collections in the United States, and since 1968 he has had over 300 one-man and group shows, at such institutions as the National Museum of American Art, the Carnegie, the National Academy of Sciences, and International Photokina. In 1979, he was one of twelve photographers invited to participate in the first photography exhibition ever held in the White House. Ketchum received his B.A. *cum laude* from UCLA and an MFA in photography from California Institute of the Arts.

Other contributors: Kim Collavo, Ellen Easton, J.R. Eyerman, Ganna Walska Lotusland Archives, A.L. Gardner, Amy Holm, Karl Obert, Stephen G. Schott, Arden Stevens, Arthur C. Sylvester, Steven Timbrook, the Hania P. Tallmadge Collection

Photographer Credits

Wm. B. Dewey: (© Photographs 1995 Wm. B. Dewey) back cover (all), pps. 1, 2, 4, 6, 8-9 (spread) 11T, 14, 16C, 17BR, 21TL & TR, 22TC & BL, 23, 24-25, 26 (all), 28 TC &BR, 29 TR, 31, 33 BL, 34 (all), 35TC, 37, 38L, 39R, 42 (all), 45 (all), 46L, 51, 54TL, BL & BR, 55, 56L, 57R, 58, 60-61 (all), 64-66(all), 68B, 70TL, 71 T & B, 72BL, 74L, 77, 79, 80TL, TC, TR & BL, 82-84, 86 TR & BR, 88-90 (all), 92 TL & TR, 93, 94 TR & BL, 95, 96B, 98, 100 TL, 101, 102 TR, 103, 104T, 121R, 126 BR, 127BL, 133R, 135BL, 136 TL, CL, BL, 140TL

Gregory L. Padgett: (Photographs © 1995 Gregory L. Padgett) front cover, pps. 7, 10, 15, 22CL & BR, 27, 29 TL, BL, & BR, 32 BC, 33 TL & C, 35TL & TR, 38R, 39L, 43, 44, 48- 50, 54TR, 62- 63(all), 67, 70BR, 71C, 72T & 72-73 (spread), 75, 76, 78, 80BR, 81L, 85R, 86 TL & BL, 91, 92 BL, C, BR, 99, 100BR, 102 TL, 105, 106B, 111B, 119, 120TL, 127TR & BR, 130, 133C, 134 (all), 140TC, 144

Robert Glenn Ketchum: (Photographs © 1995 Robert Glenn Ketchum) pps. 3, 12, 13, 32TL, 35B, 40-41 (spread), 46R, 52, 53, 56-57 (spread), 59 (all), 69, 87, 97, 104B, 120-121 (spread),126 TL, 131, 132L, 136-137 (spread)

Ganna Walska Lotusland Archives: pps. 8-9 (spread) 16T & B(Both The Arden Stevens Collection), 17T, 17BL (Photo by Gollinge courtesy of Joan and Palmer Jackson), 17BR, (photo by Karl Obert) 18T, 18B(courtesy of Joan and Palmer Jackson), 19 (photo by Shreve Ballard), 20 (TR The Arden Stevens Collection), 21B(courtesy of Joan and Palmer Jackson), 28 BL, 28TR (photo by Arthur C. Sylvester) & 28CR, 30 (all), 36 (all), 68T (painting by Coles Phillips), 106 (v, vi), 108, 110 (110TR photo by Palmer, 110B, photo by Weld), 112-115, 116L, 117, 122T, 124(all), 125C, 128-129, 132B, 132R, 133L (photo by Jay Steffy), 142 (The Arden Stevens Collection), 143 (photo by Karl Obert)

Hania P. Tallmadge Collection: pps. 106 (i, photo by Mishkin, NY, ii, iii , iv), 107, 109, 110 TL, 111, 112 (ii and iv), 114 B, 116R, 118 (118T, photo by Bachrach), 122B, 123R (photo by Lowy)

Steven Timbrook: pps. 71C, 85L, 94 TL & BR, 96TL & TR, 102 BL & BR

J.R. Eyerman: pps. 28BL, 124TR, 128, 132B

Stephen G. Schott: pps. 28TL, 47, 74R, 127TL

The Arden Stevens Collection: 16T &B, 20TR, 142

Kim Collavo: pps. 5, 32TR, 81R

A.L. Gardner: pps. 125TL & BR, 135BR

Karl Obert: pps. 17BR, 143

Ellen Easton: pg. 11B

Amy Holm: pg. 140TR

Arthur C. Sylvester: pg. 28TR

> *Key*
> T = top TL = top left TC = top center TR = top right C = center
> CL = center left CM = center middle CR = center right B = bottom
> BL = bottom left BC = bottom center BR = bottom right. If pictures are in a row, they are labeled from left to right as i, ii, iii, iv, and so on.

(Photographs copyrighted by each named photographer or organization)

Library of Congress Cataloging-in-Publication Data

Gardner, Theodore Roosevelt.
    Lotusland : a photographic odyssey / text by Theodore Roosevelt Gardner II. -- 1st ed.
      p. cm.
    Includes bibliographical references (p.   ) and index.
    ISBN 0-9627297-5-2 (alk. paper)
    1. Lotusland (Santa Barbara, Calif.) 2. Lotusland (Santa Barbara, Calif.)--Pictorial works. 3. Walska, Ganna. I. Title.
SB466.U7L694 1995
712'.6'0979491--dc20   95-14944
                                                                         CIP

Copyright © 1995
photo copyright © by Kim Collavo, Wm. B. Dewey, Ellen Easton, J.R. Eyerman, Ganna Walska Lotusland Archives, A.L. Gardner, Amy Holm, Robert Glenn Ketchum, Karl Obert, Gregory Padgett, Victoria Roberts, Stephen G. Schott, The Arden Stevens collection, Arthur C. Sylvester, Hania P. Tallmadge and Steven Timbrook
text copyright © by Theodore Roosevelt Gardner II

First published in the U.S.A. by
Allen A. Knoll, Publishers
200 West Victoria Street
Santa Barbara, CA 93101
Second Impression 1996

All rights reserved. No part of this book may be reproduced or transmitted in any form or by any means, electronic or mechanical, including photocopying, recording, or by any information storage and retrieval system, without permission in writing from the Publisher.

*Typeface: Text: Electra 2 Old Style Face, 12 point
Titles: Bauer Bodoni Titling
printed on 150 gsm glossy stock, smythe sewn, 3-piece binding, printed in Singapore by Dai Nippon Printing*

Research by Sharon Crawford
Production by A.B. Gale
Text by Theodore Roosevelt Gardner II
Copy Editor: Elaine Cappleman
Plant Identification: Virginia Hayes (general)
                            Robin Primich (Aloes)

Acknowledgments

With gratitude to the Lotusland Foundation Staff for opening their archives to us, and for not withholding any information that might have inhibited the telling of the Ganna Walska story.

The thoughts and viewpoints expressed in this book as well as the selection and presentation of material are those of the author alone. No sanction, endorsement or agreement of the Lotusland Foundation is intended or implied.

Among the sources consulted for this work were the following:

Personal Interviews: Hania Tallmadge, William Paylen, Loran M. Whitelock, Gregory Padgett
Interview documents: Frank Fujii, Patricia Tarkowska, Oswald da Ros, William Paylen, Patricia Patricia Cleek, Margaret M. Griffin
Video tape: Dr. Warren Austin
Memoir: Charles Glass, Kinton B. Stevens, Ralph T. Stevens
Ganna Walska's Books: *Always Room at the Top*, (Richard R. Smith Publ, NY) *My Life with Yogi* (manuscript)
Recording of Ganna Walska singing
The Letters and telegrams to Ganna Walska: Dr. Joseph Fraenkel, Harold McCormick, Theos Bernard, Irma and Christian Rub, Pearl Chase, Lockwood de Forest, Phelan Beale, Charles Glass, Julien Francis Goux
Letters from Ganna Walska to: Orpet Nursery, Irma and Christian Rub, Baroness Alexandra Fredericks (sister of Arcadie D'Einghorn), Mrs. A.V. Crowninshield
Historical Symbolism of the Lotus: Janet M. Eastman
A transcript of a purported newspaper interview by Robert Murry, which could be spurious
Books: Erté: *Things I Remember* 1975, pp. 53-56
Birmingham, Stephen *The Grandes Dames* 1982 "Mrs. McCormick Departs," Chapter 13.
Magazine Articles:
Musical America, December 15, 1928, "Mephisto's Musings: Ganna Walska Challenges and Makes a Debut."
Time Magazine, Volume XII, No. 25, December 17, 1928, p. 48, Music: In Binghamton, Walska."
The Musical Leader, Vol. 56, No. 8, February 21, 1929, "Ganna Walska Crowds Carnegie Hall."
Newsweek, September 6, 1943, pp. 92, 94, "Ganna Walska's Calvary," (a review of her published book, *Always Room at the Top*).
Trees Magazine, Vol. 15, No. 5, July-August 1955, pp.8, 18, "'Lotus Land' the Madame Ganna Walska Estate in Santa Barbara," by Margaret Mellinger Griffin.
Principes, October 1967, Vol. 11, No. 4, pp. 123-130, "The Palms at Lotusland," by Barry L. Osborne.
The Cactus & Succulent Journal (U.S.), Vol XLIV, Nov Dec 1972, No. 6 pp. 246 251, "Lotusland and the Fabulous Garden of Mme Ganna Walska," by Charles Glass and Bob Foster.
The Cactus & Succulent Journal (U.S.), Vol. XLVI, No 2, pp. 72-73; No. 3, pp. 120-121; and No. 4, pp. 151-152, 1974, "The Succulents of Lotusland," (in 3 parts) by Charles Glass and Bob Foster.
Santa Barbara Magazine, Volume 6/Number 2, Summer 1980, pp. 56-59, 62-66, "Lotusland the Estate of Madame Ganna Walska," By Annette Burden.
Pacific Horticulture, Volume 44, No. 1, Spring 1983, pp. 20-23, "Lotusland," by W. George Waters.
Horticulture, Volume LXVii, No. 12, December 1989, pp. 34-41, "Lotusland...in Santa Barbara, a surreal and dramatic landscape spells enchantment," by Rayford Reddell.
Connoisseur, October 1990, pp. 98-100, 156, "Lotusland, a first view of America's most exotic garden," by Maggie Keswick.
Santa Barbara Magazine, March/April 1991, pp. 37-38, 41, "Inside Lotusland," by Trish Reynales.
Montecito Magazine, Vol XI, No. 2, Fall 1991, pp. 28-33, 61-63, "Madame of Lotusland: Ganna Walska," by Elias Chiacos.
Elle Decor, November 1991, Vol. 2, No. 9, pp. 71-73, "The Diva's Secret Garden—Ganna Walska's Curious Landscaping," by Lisa Zuniga.
The Garden, Journal of the Royal Horticultural Society, Vol. 118, Part 2, February 1993, pp. 78-81, "Bravura Performance," by Martin Wood.

Some Garden Designers and Contractors who Contributed to Lotusland

R. Kinton Stevens, Ganna Walska, Oswald da Ros, George Washington Smith, Koichi Kawana, Frank Fujii, Peter Reidel, Paul Theine, Lockwood de Forest, Ralph T. Stevens, Charles Glass, Bob Foster, William Paylen, Dennis Shaw, Fritz Kubish, Terry Clay, Pat Scott, Sydney Baumgartner and Isabelle Greene.

INDEX

abalone shells, 6, 54, 56-57, 136-137
Acer palmatum atropurpureum, 74
Aeonium arboreum atropurpureum "Zwartkop", **43**, 71
aerial views, **20, 21**
Agapanthus orientalis, 83
Agave americana, 68
Agave franzosinii, 10, 68, **71, 127**
Aloe arborescens, 66
Aloe arborescens X ferox, 54, **60, 64**
Aloe arborescens X humilis, **65**
Aloe bainesii, **55, 60, 62, 67,** 126
Aloe candelabrum, 22, 54, **58, 60, 61**
Aloe dichotoma, 62
Aloe excelsa, 66
Aloe ferox, **61, 64**
Aloe Garden, **front cover**, **7, 22, 54-67, 94**
Aloe hybrids, 22, 54, **60, 63, 64, 65,** 66
Aloe marlothii, 22, **56, 60, 64**
Aloe mitriformis, 44
Aloe mutabilis, **63, 64, 65**
Aloe plicatilis, **59, 64, 136-137**
aloe pond, **6, 54, 56-57, 136-137**
Aloe ramosissima, **56-57**
Aloe salm-dyckiana, 54, **60, 64**
Aloe speciosa, **136-137**
Aloe spectabilis, 54, **60, 63, 64**
Aloe spinosissima, **64, 65, 127**
Aloe striata, **front cover**, 62
Aloe succotrina, 66
Always Room at the Top, 108, 109, 111, 112, 124, 129
Amazon water lily, 82
Atlas cedar, 68, **70, 71**
Australian treefern, **50, 52**
Bamboo, 20, 74
bathhouse, 81, 82, **131, 143**
Beale, Phelan, 117
Beaucarnea recurvata, 28
Beaucarnea stricta, **59**

Begonias, 48
Bernard, Theos, 110, **112,** 113, **118,** 124, 130
Blue fescue, 68
Blue Garden, **35,** 68
Blue hesper palms, **35,** 68, **69, 70, 71,** 92
Bowiea volubilis, **22**
Brahea armata, **35,** 68, **69, 71,** 92
Brahea edulis, 91
Brest-Litovak, Poland, 108
Bromeliads, **12, 23, 26, 32, 121,** 126, **131, 132, 134**
Brugmansia, **52**
Buddha statue, **119**
Burro-tail, **127**

Butia, **63,** 91, **94**
Cactus, **12,** 17, **23, 26, 32, 34-47, 128-129, 131, 132**
Cactus flower, **134**
Calabanis hookeri, 68, **70, 71**
carved totem, **133**
Cedrus atlantica cv. glauca, 68, **70, 71**
Cephalocereus senilis, **23, 34, 35, 36,** 38
Cereus peruvianus, **128**
Ceratozamia, **105**
Chicago Light Opera House, 116

Chicago Opera Company, 113, 116
Chilean wine palms, 3, 16, **17,** 60, **67,** 92, **93, 94,** 126, 132
Chusquea coronalis, **74**
Clarke, Humphrey, 20, 21
Climbing onion, **22**
clock, **28**
Cochran, Alexander Smith, **112,** 113, 115, 116
concrete statues, **30-31, 34, 35, 133**
coral, **44**
Cross, John, 21
Cuesta Linda, **18,** 20, 21
Cupressus macrocarpa, 26, **95**
Cycads, **8-9,** 14, **96-105, 120-1, 130,** 134
Cycas revoluta, 74, **77**
Cymbidium, **29**
d'Einghorn, Arcadie, 108, **112,** 113
de Forest, Lockwood, 132
Dioon, **99, 101, 102**
Dioon spinulosum, **100, 135**
Dracaena draco, 26, **35, 46, 93**
Dragon trees, 26, **35, 46, 93**
Eastman, Janet, 81, 86
Eaton, Charles, 21

Echeveria, **42, 70, 71**
Echinocactus grusonii, **1, 24-25, 35, 36, 45, 128**
Eichhornia crassipes, 81
Encephalartos, **99, 101, 102, 104**
Encephalartos arenarius, **96**
Encephalartos altensteinii, **97**
Encephalartos friderici-guilielmi, **102**
Encephalartos lehmannii, **102, 120-121**
Encephalartos paucidentatus, **104**
Encephalartos pteregonus, **104**
Encephalartos transvenosus, **102**
Encephalartos woodii, **8-9, 96,** 97, **102, 104**
Epicactus species, **127**
Epiphyllum, **133**
Euphorbia, 34, **35, 40-41**
Euphorbia horrida, **40-41**
Euphorbia ingens, **1, 13, 24-25, 26, 35, 38, 39, 128**
Euphorbia obovalifolia, **40-41, 46**
Euphorbia resinifera, **46**
fern gardens, 35, **48-53**
Festuca ovina v. glauca, 68
fish statue, **85**
fountain, **29, 32**
Fraenkel, Joseph, Dr., **112,** 113, **114**
French château, 30
fruit orchard, 32
Furcraea roezlii, 92
Gabor, Zsa Zsa, 112
Ganna Walska Lotusland Foundation, 21
Gavit, Erastus Palmer, **18,** 21
Giant chain fern, 48
Glass, Charles, 131
Golden barrel cactus, **1, 24-25, 35, 36, 45, 128**
Grindell-Matthews, Harry, **112,** 117
Heavenly bamboo, 74
Historical symbolism of the lotus, 81, 86

Page numbers with photographs are in bold type

Horowitz, Vladimir, 109
house, 1, 9, 13, 19, 24-25, 26, 28, 32, 33, 34, 35, 39, 40-41, 95, 132
Howea forsteriana, 91, 94, 120
Idria columnaris, 17
International Harvester Company, 116
Jacques, Burkill, 21
Jade, **34**
Japanese black pine, 74
Japanese Garden, 22, **72-79**, 82
Japanese maple, 74
Japanese pond, 17, 72, 73, 74, 76, 77, 79, **134**
Johnson, Reginald, 26
Jubaea chilensis, 3, 16, 17, 60, 67, 92, 93, 94, **126**, 132
Kalanchoe beharensis, **35**
Kalanchoe fedtschenkoi, **42**
Kentia palms, 91, 94, **120**
Knapp, George Owen, 21
lawn area, 32, **33**
lemon arbor, 28
Lemon trees, 16, 17
Lepidozamia peroffskyana, 100, **103**
Livistona, 91
Livistona chinensis, **92**
Los Angeles County Museum of Art, 124, 125
Lotus, 4, 11, 15, 16, 17, 72, 74, 75, 80, 82, 83, 86, 87, **88-89**, 119, 121, 134, **136**, back cover
Lotus Pond, 16, 18, 22, 77
"Lotusland" (in succulents), **129**
"Lotusland" signs, **11**, **135**
Macrozamia, 105
Madame Butterfly, 22, 74, 76, 124
Mammillaria, **35**
Maufair, M.A., 21
McCormick, Harold, **112**, 113, 115, **116**
metate, **99**
Montecito, 16, 17, 18
Monterey cypress, 26, **95**
mosaic path, 28
Mother in-law's cushion, 1, **24-25**, **35**, **36**, 45, **128**

Murray, Robert, 112
My Life With Yogi, 112
Myrtillocactus geometrizans, **35**
Nandina domestica, 74
Nelumbo cultivar, 22, **83**, 89
Nelumbo lutea, 88
Nelumbo nucifera, 4, 11, 15, 22, 72, 78, 80, 82, 83, 84, 86, 87, **88-89**, 119, 121, 134, **136**, back cover
Neobuxbaumia polylopha, 25, **38**
Neoregelia, **32**
neptune fountain, **32**
New York Metropolitan Opera, 118
Newbold, Charles, 21
Night-blooming *Cereus*, **39**
Night-blooming white flower, 82
Notocactus leninghausii, 34, **36**, **37**
Nymphaea caerulea, 82
Nymphaea lotus, 82
Oak trees, 18, 26, **127**
Old man cactus, **23**, 34, **35**, **36**, **38**
Olea europaea, 28
olive allée, 18, 32
Pachypodium lamierei, 68, **71**
Paderewski, Madame and Mr., 112
Palms, **56-57**, **90-94**, 134
Papyrus, 3, 86
parterre, 32, **33**
pavilion, 21, 26, 29, 34, **45**
Phoenicophorium borsigianum, 91

Phoenix, 91
Phoenix canariensis, 90
Phoenix reclinata, 33, **59**, 95
Pilosocereus, **35**
Pinus thunbergiana, 74, 76
plant societies, 133
Platycerium bifurcatum, **53**
Podocarpus elatus, 3
Poland, 108, 111
Ponytail palms, 28
Pritchardia, 91
Puacz, Hanna, 108, 109
Puacz, Carolina and Napolean, 108
Purple scallops, **42**
Puya laxa, **42**
Quercus agrifolia, **12**, 26
Rhyopalostylis sapida, **92**
rose garden, 27, 32, **33**
Royal water lily, 82
Rub, Christian and Irma, 109, 133
Sabal, 91
Sago palm, 74, **77**
Salix babylonica, 74
San Francisco Golden Gate Park, 18
Sedum morganianum, **127**
sixteenth-century globes, **127**
Smith, George Washington, 5, 26
Sphaeropteris cooperi, **50**, **52**
Straram, Walther, 116
St. Petersburg, 54

Staghorn fern, **49**, **53**
Stenocereus marginatus, **34**
Stevens, R. Kinton, 16, 26, 91, 132
Stevens, Caroline, 16
Stevens, Ralph T., 18
Stevensonia grandiflora, 91
succulent garden, **68**, **127**
swans, **76**
Syagrus romanzoffiana, 90
Sycamore Canyon Road, 10, 16, **17**, 130
Tallmadge, Hania Puascz, 124
Tanglewood, 16, 18, 21
theater garden, 30
Théâtre des Champs Elyseés, 112, 116, 117
Tibetland, 20, 21, 80, **118**
tile fountain, **29**
topiary animals, 28
Torii gate, **75**
Trichocereus, 26, **39**
Trichocereus terscheckii, **47**
Tridacna clam shells, **cover**, **56-57**, **62**
Varigated pineapple, **23**, **32**
Victoria regia, 82
Victoria regia cv. Longwood, **2**, **85**
Walnut orchard, 32
Walska, Ganna, 16, 20, 21, 22, 26, 28, 30, 32, 34, **48**, 54, **58**, **68**, 74, 76, 80, 81, 86, 91, 97, 99, **106-111**, 112, **122**, **123**, 124-125, **128-131**, **132-133**, 134, 135, **144**
    collections, 122, **124**
    marriages, 106, 11, 111, **112-118**
    opera career, 22, 74, 108, 110
    perfume, 123
    will, 134
Washingtonia filifera hybrid, **24-25**, 90
Water Gardens, 3, **5**, 80, 81, **85**, 86, 87
Water hyacinth, 81
water stairs, 18, **81**,
Water lily (hardy), 88
water lily ponds, 81, 82, 84, 86
Weeping willow tree, 74
whaling pot, **29**
"White Lama", 80, 118
Woodwardia fimbriata, **48**

IN MEMORY OF GANNA WALSKA
1887-1984